MW00441499

My Life Across the Table

Eddie Daniels at The Little Room Studio

About the Author

Karen Page is a renowned professional psychic with more than forty years of experience. Her U.S. and international clients include heads of state, CEOs of major corporations, celebrities, law-enforcement professionals, individuals, couples, and families. Regularly featured on national radio and TV programs, with guest appearances on numerous daytime television shows, Karen has hosted syndicated radio programs broadcast across the country. She lives in Southern California.

My Life Across the Table

Stories from a Psychic's Life

Karen Page

Llewellyn Publications
Woodbury, Minnesota

FIRST EDITION
First Printing, 2013

Book design by Donna Burch
Cover art: Background: iStockphoto.com/mcswin
         Crystal ball: Pete Gardner/Photographer's Choice/PunchStock
Cover design by Adrienne Zimiga
Interior art by Llewellyn Art Department

Llewellyn Publications is a registered trademark of Llewellyn Worldwide Ltd.

Library of Congress Cataloging-in-Publication Data (Pending)
ISBN: 978-0-7387-3581-8

Llewellyn Worldwide Ltd. does not participate in, endorse, or have any authority or responsibility concerning private business transactions between our authors and the public.

All mail addressed to the author is forwarded but the publisher cannot, unless specifically instructed by the author, give out an address or phone number.

Any Internet references contained in this work are current at publication time, but the publisher cannot guarantee that a specific location will continue to be maintained. Please refer to the publisher's website for links to authors' websites and other sources.

Llewellyn Publications
A Division of Llewellyn Worldwide Ltd.
2143 Wooddale Drive
Woodbury, MN 55125-2989
www.llewellyn.com

Printed in the United States of America

I dedicate *My Life Across the Table* to my mother.
If I had not been blessed enough
to have her as my mother,
I surely would have chosen her as my friend.

Contents

Introduction

I have been a professional psychic for more than forty years. Over the years I have been very blessed to live and work with people from almost every walk of life, and to read for people from just about every country, culture, and faith. When asked what I do, I tell people that "I have the most interesting job in the world, because no two people's lives are ever alike."

Every time a client says, "Wow! Karen, I've been coming to you for readings now for over thirty years or more," I still find it profound and amazing, and have always believed that my extraordinary psychic gifts are truly a "gift from God."

My work is about the lives of everyone—from deeply personal issues such as marriages, divorces, and substance abuse in families and with loved ones, to helping CEOs make corporate decisions. I have predicted many marriages and then danced at them, and I have predicted many babies and then been blessed to become a part of their lives, too. I wouldn't change a moment of it, because what I have shared and learned from my work is priceless.

I advise many large corporations that started with the seed of an idea when the CEOs and I met, and I continue to guide them through their growth with large and small decisions in the ever-changing environment of global business. I have worked with just about everyone: from homicide detectives in Europe, the United States, and Latin America to members of the British parliament in London. For many years I have given readings to leaders of Japanese media, bankers in Brazil, record-company presidents, world-famous entertainers, high-ranking politicians in the United States and abroad, housewives, rocket scientists, lawyers, contractors, movie stars, and artists.

Every single individual who has come to me holds a very special place in my heart, and I am humbled and honored to share in their lives so intimately. I feel blessed every day by my work, helping my clients by touching their lives, healing their pain, and opening spiritual doors they didn't know existed.

I have had the privilege to influence tens of thousands of people, dramatically impacting their lives for the better by guiding them through the obstacles of life, and opening their hearts and their minds to a life so fresh with possibilities each day.

I didn't know that my extraordinary gifts of seeing, knowing, and feeling things about everyone and everything were not shared, understood, or welcomed by everyone. The reality of that message was very painful, and clearly delivered to me by a group of girls I tried to fit in with, not long after entering junior high. Their cruelty was surprising to me even then. It didn't take me very long to realize that they couldn't possibly understand that the information I knew about people and their lives has always been like breathing for me, or knowing what color my eyes are.

Whether I have met someone face to face or have just heard their name, I have always known what was currently going on and what was going to happen, and I was born with insight into people's lives and circumstances. In many readings there will be long-term predictions of five or ten years before an event occurs. Such readings have provided very specific signposts, helping clients become aware of upcoming issues or events along the way.

I was born and raised in Los Angeles. I grew up around my Aunt Dorothy, a spiritual reader for over fifty years, and my mother's friend Rachel, a card reader. My childhood "gift of sight" was very clear to everyone except me. In my early teens I was introduced to the legendary psychic Peter Hurkos, who in 1964 had worked on the Boston Strangler case, and psychic and astrologer Jeane Dixon, who had famously predicted the assassination of President John F. Kennedy. On sight they recognized and nurtured my psychic gifts, helping me to grow as a person and teaching me to trust what I saw in my readings. Over the years Peter and Jeane exhibited a deep and abiding trust in my gift, repeatedly referring many of their longtime clients to me for readings. We remained good friends for the remainder of their lives.

It started out with simple things in everyday conversations, no big revelations. Then, quite literally, no matter who I was talking to, I would unconsciously start giving them a reading, as my gift took over every word that came out of my mouth. I couldn't help but notice the startled looks on people's faces after a ten- or fifteen-minute conversation. They would stare at me and say, "How did you know that?" I was already very shy, so freaking people out just by talking was driving me crazy. I had no idea how weird this was for people, to meet some young girl who knew intimate details about them and spoke to them like she was living their life.

I was just being myself without realizing that whatever I was saying was completely unnerving to almost every person I spoke with. I couldn't open my mouth without predictions falling out. Whether it was about someone's life or the world in general, I couldn't imagine what was happening to me and what I was supposed to "do" with all of the information I was receiving about people.

When I was twelve, I was recommended to a reader who had repeated many of the predictions I had made to a mutual friend over breakfast. She finally put a name to what was going on with me. She told me that I was a psychic, and that I would be doing "The Work." I came to find out that "The Work" meant I would be giving readings, and that my life's work would be in spiritual practices. I was sure she was wrong.

I had been around psychics since I took my first breath, and I thought that I knew what a psychic was. My readings were nothing like my Aunt Dorothy's or my mother's friends', or the way my mother's intuition was exhibited—and though I had already started giving readings, the only people I would even agree to read for were other psychics, because I absolutely refused to accept the fact that being a psychic was "God's plan" for me.

Shortly thereafter, my world simply fell apart. Major health, family, and money issues engulfed every part of my life. Finally, I asked God if He was mad at me. The answer came through a friend when she said, "Karen, you keep asking God to show you the door. You are standing in it! Open your eyes!"

It was the beginning of my life.

Over the years, I came to understand why for so many years throughout my childhood I had simply refused to accept that I was psychic. Because my gift has always been there and it is all I have ever known, the information about other people's lives has never come to me like a bolt out of the blue, or watching a television screen, or some other unusual, out-of-the-normal experience. When a client calls for an appointment and sits across the table from me, it is as though I quietly step into their life for the duration of their reading. I have always described what a reading feels like for me as "being there" with the client, in the client's life. I see what the client sees and will see, feel what they feel and will feel, and experience what they are experiencing and will experience. I am not looking at something outside of myself. It is as though I am right beside them, seeing and experiencing what they are seeing and experiencing. In great detail I am seeing and feeling whatever they are going through, whether it is from the past, the present, or the future of their lives.

I am forever amazed at the details that are revealed in my readings. When I see a person in a reading that my client will meet, regardless of whether it is business or personal, I will see where that person is from, what they sound like, if they have an accent or speak another language, their education level, how they dress and carry themselves, and if they are married, separated, or divorced. I will see if they have siblings, and how many, if they have children, and how many, and even if their parents are alive, where they live, and the nature of their familial relationships—and, most important in a reading when other people appear, I will see what the person's intention and purpose is in my client's life.

I believe everyone has God-given gifts. Some people are gifted with the ability to paint, and some to write, sing, or dance. Others are blessed with a talent to teach, to parent, or to heal. Seeing, knowing, and feeling are some of my gifts, and recognizing my psychic gifts and the responsibilities that come with them has opened doors for spiritual growth throughout my life that I share with you in this book.

My Life Across the Table is a collection of true stories inspired by clients and experiences that have touched my life in ways I could not have dreamed possible.

This book has taken me many years to write, because every one of the stories that I have selected represents a deeply personal experience in my life—people and experiences that have affected me profoundly and have helped me grow spiritually, as a psychic and as a person. Please remember that I am human, too, and although I have an innate ability to "see, know, and feel," I am still awed, surprised, inspired, and sometimes shocked to my very core from my experiences.

I have found myself giving readings in every conceivable location, for my seatmate on an airplane to a conversation in the aisle of a grocery store, but most often I give readings in my dining room. I usually sit, in what has always been referred to as "the psychic's chair," at a small, round dining table with a continuously filled coffee mug and a bottle of water at my side. My friends and clients know this table intimately, and I consider myself very lucky that the table in my dining room can't talk!

I share my stories with you to help bring awareness to my world as a psychic, to help demystify the false prophecies, and to help you understand that we are not alone in this journey through life. There is a higher power that we can all connect with and that resonates through all of us.

Every one of us has a purpose in this life, and a destiny to fulfill in our lifetime here on Earth. While certain parts of our lives are fated or destined, I have always believed that we are born with free will and the opportunity to make choices, or have control over many of the issues in our lives. My purpose in this life is delivered clearly through every reading. It is to help guide my clients to a better understanding of their free-will choices and what is destined along their journey in life.

When I was writing this book, my wish was for you to take away something from my deeply personal stories. I hope you learn to look at yourself, your life, your spirituality, and the world around you through different eyes, in a new light of possibilities.

I have changed my clients' names to protect their privacy, but every one of the people, experiences, and stories in this book are true, and they each hold a permanent place in my heart.

When I first started giving readings, I didn't realize the sheer nature of the work nor could I have known the lifelong emotional and spiritual impact my clients and their stories would have on my life.

These stories have taught me many lessons about life, and I carry within me a clear and certain knowing that there is a plan for every one of us. I know that, without exception, every single person has a personal journey leading them to their destiny.

I wish for you to find many things in these stories. I wish for you to find the gifts of an open mind, spiritual growth, and self-acceptance, because none of us is perfect; we are not supposed to be, so allow yourself to be human. If you are in pain or in trouble, ask for guidance, and know with certainty that it will be available when you need it the most. Be open, because it may not come in the package you expected—but when it arrives, have gratitude and listen with your heart.

I hope you enjoy the stories I have chosen to share, and that in some small way they can convey the impact and importance of the work in a psychic's life. I live in gratitude every day for having been entrusted and blessed with an extraordinary gift, and for the opportunity to live this amazing life.

I hope that you learn to trust your instincts and to listen to that still, small voice that lives within us all, and that someday you will join me across the table.

My Life

When I was growing up, I thought everyone was just like me. I thought they just knew things in the same "certain" way that I did. Though I was very shy, from the time I was three or four years old I always tried to tell my mother what I saw.

When I was a little girl, we lived across the street from the Willinsale family. They lived in a beautiful two-story home and appeared to be a happy, close-knit family. One day I was staring out of our living room window looking at the Willinsale house, when out of nowhere I calmly told my mother, "Mommy, Mr. Willinsale beats his wife."

At my side in an instant, and visibly upset, my mother held me close, sure that I didn't have any idea what I was saying. "That's a terrible thing to say, sweetheart," she said. "I don't know where that came from, but don't say things like that, okay?"

Though I knew my words had upset my mother, the clarity of what I saw, and the certainty I felt, didn't change. "I'm sorry, but it's true, Mommy. Mr. Willinsale beats his wife."

I didn't bring it up again, not even three weeks later when an ambulance and a police car pulled up in front of the Willinsale home. Within a few minutes, the two teenaged Willinsale children came out, huddled together, and stood sobbing in their driveway. Mrs. Willinsale, with bandages on her face, was brought out on a stretcher and lifted into the ambulance. A few minutes later, a handcuffed Mr. Willinsale, flanked by two police officers, emerged from the house and was placed in the back of the police car.

After this particular experience, my mother realized I was seeing something that she could not, and she began to understand that when I said something this specific, it was important to me. I had always been a serious child, and she knew that I would never just make something up, nor would I ever lie. If I felt, saw, or knew something, it usually came with a lot of details that, at three or four years old, I definitely had no way of knowing. After Mr. Willinsale's arrest, she never admonished me again for telling her what I felt or saw, no matter how unlikely it may have sounded or difficult it was for her to hear. I just looked at the world through very different eyes.

My mother and my aunt were incredibly psychic, as well as my mother's two closest friends, so I grew up in a family that was comfortable with people knowing things they had no logical way of knowing. My mother was a businesswoman, and though she never developed her gift or gave readings, she possessed an uncanny intuitive ability. She always just knew stuff about people that she shouldn't have known. If she mentioned someone out of the blue that she hadn't seen or heard from in years, I could be sure they would show up or call within two hours!

My Aunt Dorothy was a reader for over fifty years. She gave readings to longtime private clients, and she opened one of the first metaphysical centers in Los Angeles. Aunt Dorothy's tool was what are called *billets*. They are questions written on a small piece of paper and sealed in an envelope. The reader holds the envelope, never reading the question until after it is answered. It's what Johnny Carson's character "Carnac" spoofed on his show. Only when Aunt Dorothy picked up an envelope with a question in it, she really *did* know the answer, and if she made a prediction, you could count on it.

I watched her pick up those little envelopes a thousand times over the years, making accurate predictions about divorces, jobs, and unexpected pregnancies—sometimes to the surprise and often to the delight of the client. I loved watching her work, effortlessly pulling "psychic rabbits" out of her hat. She had always been completely at home with her gift, and she never ceased to amaze me.

She understood my ongoing wistful wonder of, "Oh, Aunt Dorothy, I wish I could do that."

She always reassured me, no matter how many times I said it. With a mischievous smile, she softly patted my hand. "Don't worry, sweetheart, your day will come," she'd say, adding a tender squeeze for emphasis.

I was born serious, and thought deeply about everything, so starting early in life I repeatedly heard, "Don't worry, sweetheart, just remember: 'Man plans, and God *un*plans.'" Those simple yet profoundly true words became indelibly etched upon my heart, to become the greatest advice my mother ever gave me.

When I was about eight years old, I was having lunch with my mother at our dining room table when she asked me what I wanted to be when I grew up. I thought about the question for quite a while, carefully examining all of my choices before putting my wishes into words. Even at my tender age, I understood how the power of words and choice could impact a life. I knew words carried within them the innate ability to love you or hurt you, so throughout my life I have been conscious to choose my words with great care.

I turned everything over and over in my young mind, finally coming to a decision about my future. With the naiveté and drama that only a small child can possess, I announced my carefully thought-out decision to my mother. "Mommy, when I grow up, if I can touch just one person's life and make it better, then I could die tomorrow and I would be happy."

My mother knew how serious those words were in my small world, and as much as I could comprehend them, she knew I meant every word. She also knew that I was a little girl who nurtured many big dreams.

I was such an oddball in elementary school; I was the weird, quiet girl who just "knew stuff." I was forever picked on and bullied, but I would never fight back for myself. Yet God help the bullies if they attacked one of the other kids or went after one of the teachers. That was when I would step out of my shell, with boxing gloves on.

Only an altruistic little girl like me would believe I could protect people by becoming a lawyer. Yes, this is where you laugh. You see, I thought that lawyers could just magically put away the bad guys, and that the job of a lawyer was to protect the innocent.

Please remember, I was only eight years old. Though I must confess, I quite naively nurtured that dream well into adulthood.

Of course, I hadn't lived any of those realities yet, so for a couple of years from about eight to ten, I consciously thought of myself as the normal one in my family. The one who didn't possess the abilities and gifts exhibited by almost everyone I knew; and because I was the normal one, I would have a normal job and become a lawyer.

During this time I became conscious of something else. I would be having a normal, casual conversation with someone, never realizing that I had said something personal to the other person. Something they had never revealed. Not until I saw the look on the person's face did I realize that I must have done it again. I must have said something that I clearly had no right to know.

This was my normal, everyday life, and most of the time I never thought that any of it was unusual or strange. I was too young to comprehend what the word *psychic* actually meant, or the responsibilities that come along with it.

Although I was still a child, I possessed a clear understanding of the power of words and could certainly see, and feel, the impact my words were having on others. I hadn't lived enough to understand exactly what this was, or the impact of it on my life and on those around me, though I could definitely see the reaction people had when I spoke to them. They were either intrigued or frightened by a child with deeply personal knowledge of their life. How could a little girl possibly know that a certain woman's husband had just lost his job, or that another woman's mother-in-law was in the hospital with diabetes-related issues?

I began to realize that I was making people uncomfortable. What I saw came out effortlessly in conversation, never feeling even slightly uncomfortable to me, but clearly it was to others. I briefly thought that maybe I was losing my mind.

The things I knew about people were personal and came to me clearly, and in great detail. Sometimes it was what someone was going through emotionally or physically in life, and at other times it was predictive in nature.

One day my mother's friend Linda came by for lunch. From the moment she walked in the door, she was talking about how excited she was to have gotten her first brand-new car. I was very happy for her, and though I heard what she said, all I could see in my mind were the tires. I had a terrible feeling that there was a serious problem with the left front tire on her brand-new car.

I grew up in a pretty open-minded home for the early 1960s, and naturally being a part of my mother's friendships was the way I was raised. Now I realize how progressive my mother really was. She was very big on us learning respect, and though she was open-minded, that was taught hand in hand alongside the "children should be seen but not heard" rule. Because I was relatively articulate for a small child, and never really spoke baby talk, my mother's friends always included me in their conversations.

The foreboding feeling I had about Linda's tire needed to be dealt with, and I knew I had to find a way to tell her without alarming her or upsetting my mother. I couldn't get it off my mind, and didn't say anything until she was almost out the front door. Standing next to my mother as Linda gave me a goodbye hug, I said, "Linda, I know this sounds crazy, but before you get back on the freeway, will you please have your left front tire checked?"

She smiled to reassure me. "Oh, it's a brand-new car, Karen. Thank you, but there's nothing wrong with the tires."

I was a little girl and knew that at that moment, she wasn't taking me seriously. She couldn't feel the sense of urgency rising within me, and though I knew I couldn't force her, I had to keep trying. I asked her to please listen, just to stop and have it checked. I pleaded with her repeatedly, until she finally gave in, promising me she would stop at the gas station around the corner before going home.

The phone rang about thirty minutes later. Linda was at the gas station having the left front tire changed. They found a big bulge on the inside of the tire wall, one that couldn't be seen with the naked eye. They told her if she had gotten on the freeway with it, she would have had a blowout.

Because my mother spent the majority of her time in a professional environment, she didn't easily share what she intuitively knew about people. Under normal circumstances, I would usually just say what I felt and saw—unless it was one of my mother's friends, and out of respect for my mother and her friends, I would think twice before saying anything.

Sometimes I would just blurt things out, and I used to say, "If it was in my head, it came out of my mouth." It is especially funny to me now, because I am so protective of people's privacy, but at the time I didn't possess the maturity to realize how sensitive some of these issues were. I was also too young to realize that just because I knew something, it didn't mean that I had to blurt it out.

During that same period, I started experiencing what I now call "breakthrough headaches," which could sometimes last for three weeks. They were pretty frightening, and appeared to come out of nowhere. My mother took me to every doctor for every possible test, but they could find nothing. The doctors said there was no medical reason for these torturous headaches, and finally pronounced that they must be migraines.

They were excruciating, yet I became very aware that after every breakthrough headache, some new element or part of my gift would open up within me and present itself. I experienced them on a relatively regular basis for the better part of thirty years. Now I get them occasionally, and when I do, I understand that another part of my gift is about to present itself.

I feel these headaches are God's way of saying, "Pay attention, Karen!" and He reveals a new element of my gift, when He knows I am ready.

When I was ten, it dawned on me that I truly was my mother's daughter, and like her, I too just "knew stuff" about people, except I never had to stop and think about it. It was and is always there.

By the time I was eleven, though it was still a confusing time for me, this odd gift of mine at least had a name. I was *psychic*. A lifetime of just knowing things, and several years of terrible headaches, didn't mean that I was losing my mind, and there was definitely nothing wrong with me. I realized that God had entrusted me with a very precious gift, and I needed to figure out what to do with it and how I could utilize it to help people.

By the time I finished elementary school, I had to acknowledge that this uncanny, laserlike way I had of knowing in detail a person, their intentions, and what was going to happen in their life was the most obvious manifestation of my gift.

With every passing year, my abilities became clearer, stronger, and strikingly more pronounced, while new ones that I never knew I had, like healing, opened up when I was ready.

I found that the more accepting and comfortable I was with my gifts, the broader they became. My *clairaudience*, or psychic hearing, became crisp and clear. My *clairsentience*, the ability to tap into a person's energy, feelings, and emotions; and my *claircognizance*, the sense of knowing and certainty, became dramatically clearer and well defined. The details that show up in a client's reading are forever astounding to me.

What I didn't know at the time was that it was only the beginning of my journey, and I was finding my way. A great peace came into my heart when I finally accepted that I had always just been this way. I finally admitted that being psychic truly was like breathing for me, and I fully embraced my gift.

Though I grew up around highly developed psychic energy, they were family. Because my gifts had manifested very differently than my mother's, my aunt's, or my mother's friends, it had taken the better part of my childhood to acknowledge that I was psychic, and to realize that I had been openly and actively psychic since I was three years old. They knew that when I stopped fighting my true nature, and truly accepted that I was simply born this way, God would know, and the universe would respond and help me find my way.

My self-acceptance opened up the world of other readers to me. Almost immediately I was introduced to a group of other psychics, and I found comfort and acceptance reading only for them, because I felt that aside from my family, they were the only ones who understood.

All psychics are eventually led to the tools that help them channel their work—tools they are psychically comfortable working with.

I have discovered over the years that the tool chest of a psychic can hold many different things, and the tools we use *can* be almost anything. They are what we focus on, to decipher what we are seeing and feeling. Some readers utilize tarot cards; others use crystals; and some stare into a crystal ball.

My tool of choice is psychometry. The literal definition of *psychometry*, according to the *Merriam-Webster* online dictionary, is "divination of facts concerning an object or its owner through contact with or proximity to the object." My personal definition is "vibrations carried through an object."

In my case, it can be a piece of jewelry, keys, a photograph, a business card, a person's voice, or simply the vibration carried within a name.

The group of other readers kept urging me to read professionally, to read for clients, but I wasn't comfortable doing that until I understood. It took two and a half years before I felt that I understood my purpose, and I agreed to see my first client at the age of fourteen.

That was many years and many, many thousands of readings ago, and I am forever grateful that God heard the prayer of a shy eight-year-old girl, and unplanned my life.

I know that the "perception" of what I do still makes some people uncomfortable, and scares others, but that has certainly never been my intention.

I do not force my work on anyone, nor do I try to convince anyone that I am psychic. Nor do I ever just walk up to people and start making predictions. And, last but not least, by the time I was about fourteen, I no longer felt the need to simply blurt things out.

I have a very powerful and peaceful relationship with God. I have not an ounce of conflict within me when it comes to my work, and I am very clear that this *is*, without question, the work that God planned for my life.

If the day ever comes that God no longer wants me to give readings, and wants me to become a house painter, I promise you I will be at Home Depot buying brushes the next morning.

Absolute Destiny

By 1981 I had happily been giving readings professionally for more than fifteen years when suddenly, through a very odd set of circumstances, I found myself owning and running a bakery.

My husband at the time was a very talented architect and builder, and in the spring of 1981 he had taken on a project to design and build a boutique bakery in Beverly Hills. He asked me to help and divided up the project, with him designing almost everything from the look and functionality of the space to the signs. I was given the task of outfitting the kitchen, so I set about ordering custom-made ovens, sinks, mixers, and every piece of top-of-the-line equipment necessary to turn this little bakery into a dream.

It was a beautiful little store with black-and-white tile-checkered floors, happy yellow walls, bright green chairs with black tables, and an eye-catching sign depicting huge fiberglass bananas falling from heaven. We were close to completing construction at the end of August; with all the permits finally in place and custom-built ovens and cabinets installed, the stainless-steel kitchen was getting the finishing touches.

We set up a lunch meeting with my husband's clients and were excited to turn over the keys, knowing how happy and thrilled the new owners would be with their beautiful bakery. Well, happy was not exactly their response, nor were they thrilled. To this day, I will never understand the reasoning behind their actions on that fateful afternoon.

Though it was odd that they had never stopped by or been around during construction, all of a sudden over lunch, and without any explanation whatsoever, they told us they didn't want the bakery. Out of nowhere and without warning, they changed their minds, ate lunch, and simply walked away. We were dumbstruck, and because my husband had never been fully paid for all of his work or the equipment, when they walked out the door, we were left owning the bakery.

My husband was definitely not going to run a bakery, and he had so many other projects going on that I was the one suddenly thrust into running this business. Now, what was I going to do with a bakery? My mother's wisdom quickly sprang to mind. Over the years I had watched this amazing woman turn many a bitter situation into something very sweet. Her lifelong endeavors had earned not only my deepest respect and admiration but also an affectionate title. I had crowned her the "Queen of Lemonade."

To this day I can hear her words: "Sweetheart, when God gives you lemons, you make lemonade. You can make it as sweet or as bitter as you like."

Well, on this particular day, I had been presented with an entire lemon grove.

Not one ever to shy away from a challenge, I decided to dive in and make this work. I was a good cook and a fine baker, so how difficult could this be? The grand opening was scheduled for September 11, 1981, so I had less than three weeks to come up with the recipes necessary to turn this into an actual, functioning bakery.

I spent the next couple of weeks in the kitchen, experimenting with all sorts of recipes and teaching myself to adapt them for larger quantities. I suddenly found myself knee-deep in flour and sugar for this unexpected chapter in my life.

We had named the business "The Banana Bread Box," so I knew I had to come up with a banana bread recipe that was exceptional and different. Since I love chocolate, I came up with an amazing chocolate-chip banana bread recipe that was pretty delicious, if I do say so myself. I quickly added different varieties of gingerbread, zucchini bread, carrot cake, and a few other tasty snacks to the menu. With recipes in hand, I ordered all the supplies and quite literally became the "Psychic Baker" overnight.

Thank God, we were immediately welcomed into the neighborhood. With a steady flow of customers eagerly enjoying my freshly baked cakes, the surprising dose of lemonade served up a few weeks earlier had become much sweeter indeed. The recent turn of events in my life didn't afford me the luxury of investing a lot of time thinking about why all of this had happened. I instinctively just kept sweetening the lemonade.

The decision on that fateful day had caused quick action and dramatic changes, which were now affecting every part of my life. My daily work schedule of many years had been turned upside down, as I went from waking up at eight or nine in the morning to see my first client of the day to waking up at one or two in the morning to get to the bakery.

Every busy day while sifting and measuring, I thought about giving readings. I didn't know how I was going to do it, but I was determined to continue my life's work, no matter what was going on in my life.

I just had to figure out where, in the bakery, I could make my clients comfortable and give readings under these conditions. I stepped back and looked at the layout.

The kitchen, service counter, tables, and chairs were all downstairs, not allowing privacy for my clients. Upstairs was a large storage room filled with packing and shipping supplies, and next to this was the office for the bakery. I rearranged the furniture in the office and brought in an extra chair. Placing it across from my desk, I found my place. It was small, but the energy was peaceful, and I knew I could make it work.

Now, would my clients come to see me in a small office, upstairs in a bakery? That was the big question.

Thank God they did, and no one ever complained. I was pleasantly surprised when many of them expressed their sincere enjoyment at this setup. They liked it when they got freshly baked cake and coffee along with their reading, and I could keep an eye on the bakery at the same time.

I have been very blessed in my life, because I truly love my work and my clients. They have come to see me regardless of where in the world I have lived and worked, and the bakery was no exception.

Over the years I have developed strong and enduring relationships with many people who initially came to me as clients. During my reign as the *Psychic Baker*, they made appointments often, continued referring their friends, and on occasion would come by just to have cake and coffee with me.

One of those lifelong friendships was with a lovely, soft-spoken gentleman with beautiful silver hair. His name was Allen Stone, but I always just called him "Al." We not only became friends who socialized often, but Al became my tax man. He would come to me for readings, both personally and professionally, a couple of times a year, and I went to him every year at tax time.

We cherished and trusted each other as friends and as professionals. Two or three times a year, he would call for an appointment, because he liked to give the gift of a reading to his friends. He would always drive them over for their appointments, which gave Al and I a chance to see each other more often and have a good chat over coffee.

One day he called, wanting an appointment for a friend of his named Steve. We set a time for the next afternoon, and I told him to bring Steve to the bakery. Al could have a snack while I was upstairs in my office giving the reading.

Arriving at the designated time, Al introduced Steve to me, and they took seats at a table near the counter. I served coffee, brought out a plate of sliced cakes, and came out from behind the counter to join them.

Steve was a nice-looking young man, tall and slim, in his mid- to late twenties. He had neatly cropped blond-streaked hair and beautiful blue eyes. Al and I talked good-naturedly for a while, easy banter between good friends, with Steve joining in when he could. They nibbled on cake, I sipped my coffee, and it was easy conversation.

During a momentary lull, Steve reached over, touching my arm, and quietly asked, "Excuse me, but may I use your restroom?"

"No problem, let me show you where it is." I got up, walking him through the kitchen and pointing to the bathroom door.

When I took my seat again at the table, Al said, "What time do you want me to pick him up, or should I just wait down here?"

My immediate change in mood didn't escape Al, as I took a deep breath, enveloping his hand in both of mine. I leaned forward, looking directly into his eyes, and in an urgent whisper said, "Al, you're not going anywhere. I want you to really hear me. Under no circumstances are you to get into a car with Steve behind the wheel."

For me to give him a warning of this kind was *very* serious and highly unusual, and he knew that I meant every word. I am not an alarmist by any stretch of the imagination and never have been. There are enough serious things in life to be concerned about, and I have always been quite clear about what they are.

There are very few things in a reading as serious as predicting a person's death. If it is "not their time," and the death can be prevented in any way, I am definitely not shy about sharing that information.

Al squeezed my hand nervously, thinking out loud, "I don't know how I'm going to do that, Karen. We're having dinner with friends this weekend, and Steve is picking me up."

I squeezed back harder, more urgently this time. "Take your own car, Al. Meet him there. Please, don't get in a car that he is driving! Now, do you understand?"

I hoped he realized that I was trying to save his life, because it definitely "wasn't his time," but it *was* Steve's, and there was nothing I could say or do to change Steve's fate. That was strictly in God's hands.

Al questioned me again. "What if I can't do that?"

I couldn't believe that he was going to make me say the words out loud. I was so upset that he wasn't taking this seriously. "Oh my God! Well, Al, if you insist on going with him, then I guess I'll just send flowers. Is that clear enough?"

I was relentless, pleading with him. "Please, Al, under *no* circumstances can you get into a car that he is driving! Please! Do you hear me?"

My frustration was front and center. "Do you get it now? I don't care what you tell him. Tell him you have to stay home and wash your dog!"

Still bewildered, Al muttered, "I don't know how I'm going to do this."

Leaving me with no other choice, I spelled it out for him. "I'm begging you, Al. I'm sorry, but Steve won't be here Monday morning!"

He didn't have time to respond. Steve came out of the kitchen, sat down, smiled at both of us, and got to the point I was dreading. "So, Karen, do you want to do my reading now?"

I looked at him, choosing my words with great care. "You know, Steve, you don't really need a reading right now. It feels like you need to go home and straighten out some of the issues in your life. If you still feel the same way about your life one week from today, come back and I'll read for you then. Is that okay?"

He didn't seem terribly surprised. "You know, Al, she's probably right. I don't really need a reading right now, but I do need to clear up some stuff. Next week would probably be better anyway, and then I'll get a reading."

I could barely look at him. I was afraid I would burst into tears, and he just wouldn't understand. I knew that this lovely young man was not going to be alive on Monday morning, and there was nothing I could do to change that fact. I knew it as certainly as I was breathing.

I also knew that when God has a plan for someone, interfering is absolutely *not* an option.

We finished our coffee and talked for a few more minutes. Warmly, Steve put out his hand. "It was really nice meeting you, Karen. I look forward to seeing you again next week."

Steve turned toward the door. "Al, I'll go get the car."

Looking at me, but responding to Steve, Al didn't move. "I'll just meet you out there."

Steve was barely out the door when my dog-with-a-bone urgency returned. I knew this was my last chance.

Pleadingly, I grabbed Al's hand, still seeing the confusion in his eyes. "Promise me you won't get into a car with him driving. Please, Al, promise me."

Staring out the door as if transfixed, he couldn't bring himself to look at me. "I promise, Karen, but I just don't understand."

Pulling his hand away without so much as a glance, Al quietly slipped out of the bakery.

All I could do now was hope that Al had heard me, and pray.

I was in the bakery Monday morning at 10 a.m. when the phone rang.

I heard Al's distinctly soft voice on the line. "Karen?"

I took a deep breath. "Are you okay?"

He could hardly form the words. "I'm fine, Karen, but this is just unbelievable. Steve is dead."

I was sad for his loss, but deeply grateful. Though clearly upset, at least Al was still alive. Cautiously, I probed further. "Can you tell me what happened, or would you rather not talk about it?"

Softly, Al continued, "No, I haven't even been to bed yet, but I *need* to tell you."

The grief was evident in his voice. "We just went to meet some friends last night for dinner, like we've done a hundred times. You know the place, Karen, on Ventura Boulevard. We had such a great time. A few drinks, some laughs; it all seemed so normal."

His disbelief enveloped every word. "I couldn't stop looking at him, Karen. I mean, all through dinner I just kept looking at him. He seemed so happy, and I know I keep saying this, but everything seemed so normal. We went out to the parking lot, joking around saying our goodbyes. His car was right behind me. It's *so* weird. He was just there, waving at me! I mean we were waving to each other as I pulled across Ventura Boulevard. I made a left, stopped at the light, and... and Steve pulled out and made a right."

His voice rose as the anguished words poured out. "I was still stopped at the light when I heard it! I swear, Karen, it couldn't have been ten seconds! I couldn't believe it! He hit seven parked cars! Seven! And wrapped his car around a telephone pole! He was dead before I even got to him."

I felt terrible for my dear friend. "I am so sorry, sweetheart. He seemed like a lovely guy, and I know you were good friends."

Loss brings out many emotions in people, especially when the loss is someone we care deeply for.

With Steve's sudden death only a few hours earlier, it triggered an avalanche of misplaced anger and blame in

Al. "Obviously not that close! I mean now I know! I know that you saved my life, but how could I *not* have known he was an alcoholic?! I should have known that, Karen! I can't believe that no one knew! Why didn't I know that?"

Spent from the pain, his words softened, now searching for an answer. "Couldn't you have told him, Karen? Couldn't you have changed it?"

Unfortunately, I intimately knew this grief. I have lost so many people whom I have loved in my life, but I know with certainty, and beyond a shadow of a doubt, they are always with me, and I am never alone.

This was a deeply painful and all-too-familiar emotion in my life. Although I had told Al that Steve was leaving, I could not tell Steve. I needed to help Al understand why and help him see Steve's life, and death, through my eyes.

Helping someone find peace over the loss of a loved one is never easy.

"Al," I said, "you know that you are very precious to me, and I know that your intention was for Steve to have a reading, but please try to understand. God's purpose of *you* being brought to me on that particular day was not for Steve. It was for you."

Again, I hoped that he could hear me. "I was given that information to protect you, and Al, I'm deeply sorry that I couldn't save Steve. I'm not God, remember? I just work here."

I could feel the pain washing over him. "I wish there was a nice way to say this to you, but Steve had been an alcoholic for many years. He could have changed his life at any time, yet he chose not to. By the time you brought him to see me, Steve didn't have a future. And as hard as this is to hear, that was *his* destiny, not *yours*."

Al sobbed openly now, as I continued softly. "Telling him what I saw would not have changed a thing. Please, try to understand. This was God's plan for Steve, not mine. He was going to die last night regardless of what anybody said to him, or did. *You* just weren't supposed to go with him."

Without question, I knew the purpose of them coming to the bakery, and it wasn't to give Steve a reading. The purpose was to give Al the *choice* to save his own life.

Over the remaining twenty-four years of our friendship, Al reminded me of the events of that fateful day. Until the day my beloved friend died, he repeatedly told people, "I may not always hear the advice most people give me, but I am grateful I listened to Karen that day. She saved my life."

I always said he listened from a different place, and that "different place" was his heart.

I can recall that urgent warning, delivered long ago in the bakery. I can see Steve's face, and hear Al's pain, as though it happened yesterday. That day changed our friendship and my life in many ways.

Al and I certainly became closer after Steve's death, and as strange as this may sound, I later delivered two other lifesaving warnings for Al that I didn't have to convince him about; he heard me the first time. He told me repeatedly over the years that I was his guardian angel.

The wonder of that day, and the impact of Steve's unalterable destiny, never left either of us. Those experiences with Al continued to reinforce what I have always believed about one's destiny or fate. Of the many life lessons I have learned over the years, there is one that stands out above the rest. I had an epiphany one day, and suddenly I understood why the everyday things that all of us experience in life, both emotionally and physically, appear to be only one of two ways. They are either relatively easy, or impossibly difficult.

If you look back over the issues throughout your life, and I mean the ones that you thought mattered, you will see that there really never was any gray area with any of them. They either came together, resolving themselves pretty easily, or there appeared to be one painful obstacle after another put in your way, stopping it and you. When I experienced that moment of clarity, it changed every day of my life. I call it my "20 to 40 percent formula for living."

I believe that 20 to 40 percent of our lives are *fated*, no matter what we think or do. The fated issues are *absolute*. No matter what attempts we make to avoid or change the outcome. If something is *absolute* in our life, it will occur no matter what.

The other 60 to 80 percent is free will. Like ordering a hamburger, we can have it our way, and pretty easily, any way we choose.

Free will is about having choices. If a client asks me about something that is *not* fated, I tell them to go ahead: don't take that job or buy that house or go out with that person again. They aren't going to miss what is destined in their life. Free-will choices do not change the destiny of a person's life.

Steve had no choices left. There was no future for me to see, because he didn't have one. If he hadn't died in a car accident on Sunday night, something else would have occurred to take his life before Monday morning.

I couldn't change what God had written for Steve, but it saddened me deeply to know that even though Steve had a wide circle of friends who loved him, not one of them knew he was an alcoholic spiraling out of control.

There are certain elements of the work that I describe as a "slap and a kiss." This is when the information I have to share is very painful or difficult, but something positive and enlightening can be born from the pain. Seeing Steve's unpreventable death was one of those. I could tell Al not to get in a car with him, but I could not save Steve. Nor could I stop Al. All I could do was tell him, but I couldn't control what he chose to do with the information.

During readings with several clients over the years, the imminent death of someone close to the client has appeared with great clarity. Though I have certainly wished that there *was* something I could do to change what I have seen, that is not what this work is.

When people come into this life and are taken early, I know that they were born on what I call a "short clock." No matter their age, their life wasn't about them. Their life was about all of the people who loved them, the people whose lives they touched.

When I counsel people in grief, and they speak of the depths of their loss, the first question I ask them is, "What did you learn from this relationship?"

I have learned from my own losses that we cry selfish tears. We are not crying for those who have passed over, because they are truly free. We miss them because of the way they made us feel, about our life and ourselves.

The less attached we can become to our grief, the clearer the impact and true purpose on our life of the person who has passed becomes. We then focus not on the way they died, but more importantly on the way they lived.

When you can truly and honestly embrace that, you clear the way for your lost loved one to let you know that their spirit is still with you, but they just can't get through your grief.

What you learn from having known them can become a lifetime gift of teaching and sharing, which keeps the person's memories and the blessings they brought into your world alive.

I have learned that destiny is absolute, and is one of the few things in life that is absolutely, 100 percent non-negotiable.

Meeting Peter Hurkos

I have never believed that people meet by accident or coincidence; I believe that everyone comes into our lives for a purpose. Whether they are there for five minutes or a lifetime, and whether you are momentarily placed in someone's path to make their day better or for them to change your life forever, people are always brought together for a reason. This story is about one of those fateful meetings. It was a meeting that became a lifelong education through friendship, to help me grow and understand the nature of my work, and to find peace within it. It was a meeting that changed my life.

My mother was very supportive of my psychic gifts and understood how important it was to me to help people.

She knew and accepted that I was psychic even before I did, and though I was a good student who went to school every day, she understood that I was going to be giving readings to clients either at home or in her store after school and before I did my homework.

I met Ken in the spring of 1969 when he was sent to me as a client. I was sixteen years old and had only been giving readings professionally for a little over two years. Ken was a twenty-seven-year-old New Yorker, not terribly tall and more round than lean, with a thick mop of jet-black hair that tumbled across his forehead. He had strikingly light green eyes that sparkled when he felt passionate about anything.

He was smart, funny, sharp-witted, and highly opinionated about everything that mattered to him. Without fail, his highly observant, edgy take on things always made me laugh. Though I was very young, and he was quite the character, there was an instant connection. He was one of the older brothers I never had, and a long and lovely friendship developed between us.

Ken owned a film storage vault. He was entrusted with highly prized film collections (some rare and some not-so-rare) that were all very precious to their owners. He lovingly kept track of and cared for these films as though they were his own.

The vaults were pretty sophisticated for their time. They were airtight, light-monitored, temperature-controlled, and guarded like Fort Knox. He explained to me that all of those precautions were taken to ensure the continued quality of the films, some of which were original prints or the only copies in existence.

As all of this happened many years before the introduction of digital applications in the film business, everything back then was shot, and stored, on 16mm, 35mm, or 70mm film. Ken's dedication to ensuring the films' survival for future generations, and his vast knowledge of films in general, was a fascinating world, far removed from my own.

My mother grew up working alongside her father in the flower business in New York. My grandfather owned six full-service flower shops in Manhattan, so my mother grew up surrounded by everything having to do with flowers.

After being a florist for many years, she was ready to do something different. The natural progression from flowers to the giftware business felt like the perfect fit. She found a beautiful corner store in Sherman Oaks, California, and in the late sixties opened The Imperial Bed, Bath and Closet Shop on Ventura Boulevard.

It was a lovely store with mirrored cabinets, glass shelves, and two big display windows that we changed every couple of weeks.

She stocked the store with unusual gift selections from all over the world, always seeking out the unique and rare. Everywhere the eye could see was filled with beautiful things for the home: from delicate porcelain figurines made in a family-owned factory in Italy, to lavishly embroidered towels and custom-colored lucite bathroom accessories that were highly innovative concepts in that era, to one-of-a-kind purple, gold, or red crystal decanter sets from Romania. The more exotic something was, the better she liked it. Word spread fast in the design business, and since there was nothing like my mother's store anywhere else in the country, she became the person to see.

My mother was initially a little cautious when I told her about Ken, but they hit it off instantly, as I knew they would, and soon he became like family. The three of us shared a deep unspoken comfort and trust. For a while, he got in the habit of stopping by the store two or three days a week to have lunch with us. It was time we all looked forward to, as the air was always filled with interesting conversation and lots of laughter.

He generously shared his world with us, and in return we taught Ken about trust, and about being open to his unrecognized spirituality.

Ken and I were always going somewhere together, even if he came by the store to pick me up, just to run film-business errands with him. There was always something to do, pick-ups and deliveries, paperwork, trips to the post office to send film off to a client. Whatever it was, I loved spending time with Ken.

On this particular day he came by the store earlier than usual to have lunch with us. We bantered back and forth, wading through the same stack of takeout menus as always, debating the merits of each one, until finally deciding the day's fare. Our roles in this "dance of the luncheon ritual" were clearly defined.

Once our decisions were final, and often without a word, my mother would take the chosen menu, dramatically dialing the number as we watched. She would carefully recite our order and, once done, replace the phone in the cradle with a great flourish. That was our cue to head for the door, with strict orders and a wink, not to return without lunch in hand.

As always, Ken opened the car door for me. As I slid into the seat, he casually asked, "After lunch I have to stop by a client's house. Want to come with me?"

I was always up for running errands with Ken, and I was with him so often that he started telling his clients that I was his assistant. Keeping him company was about the extent of my "assistant" duties, so for a "job that wasn't really a job," it was a pretty easy assignment.

I was quite conscious that they were his clients, and I rarely spoke after being introduced. The opportunity to go with Ken while he worked was a wonderful and educational experience for me. Ken knew that I would always honor our friendship and respect his relationships with his clients.

My working for Ken, in any way, became our little joke. "Of course, boss," I said, feigning an exaggerated bow. "I am your ever-ready assistant, remember?"

Starting the car, without so much as a glance in my direction, the slightest smile crossed his lips. "Good, I think you'll find this man very interesting."

It was an odd statement, because he knew that I found most of his clients pretty interesting. I had met some lovely people while picking up and delivering films with Ken, so it never entered my mind that this day and this client would be any different.

Yet Ken instinctively knew that taking me to meet *this* particular client would change my life forever.

We chatted as we picked up the food, returning to my mother's store to complete our mission. As was part of our "lunch dates with Ken," she had set plates and folded napkins and silverware in our usual places, wrapping around one corner of her desk.

We took our seats as Ken placed his hand in the bag, announcing everything he pulled out. With his usual dramatic flair, he waved the item around until a hand came up to claim it, ever so gently placing the prized item on its designated plate.

Sometimes our elaborate lunch plans resulted in cheese sandwiches on a Kaiser roll from across the street, but when Ken was there, it always turned into a special event.

Our leisurely lunch was littered with quick conversation and outbursts of laughter. I was usually the scorekeeper, and got great pleasure watching the interaction between Ken and my mother. They clearly knew how to playfully wind each other up, and when they got on the topic of their respective businesses, they were hilarious together.

Ken would share his dilemmas with employees, and storage details, and my mother shared funny stories about the occasional drama with her sometimes incredibly high-maintenance clients. To say the least, they were very entertaining together.

We finished lunch, and when I walked out the back door to dispose of our accumulated trash, Ken asked my mother if I could accompany him on his afternoon errands. She knew Ken was a trustworthy person, and that he would make sure I was safe, but out of respect he always asked her permission. It didn't matter that I had already consented to go. He wasn't taking me anywhere, ever, without my mother's approval.

I grabbed my purse, kissed my mother, and told her I would be back in an hour or so. Stepping around me, Ken leaned down and lovingly delivered a warm hug and a peck on her cheek.

For the second time that day Ken had that same little smile on his lips. I knew he had a secret, and I took the bait, knowing he wanted me to ask, "Okay, what have you been smiling about all day? I know you're dying to tell me."

Ken's smile got bigger, and the telltale twinkle in his eyes went on high. His entire energy shifted as he alternated between watching the road and looking at me. "Aren't you the least bit curious about who we are going to see?"

Now, *this* really was unusual. When calling on a client, his normal demeanor was very professional, somewhat laid-back, and usually relaxed. "Have I ever asked you who we were going to see before?"

I could see him turning it over in his mind. Slowing the car, he looked directly at me. "Well, no, you have never asked, but this client is different. He's someone I have a feeling you are supposed to know."

Ken glanced back and forth between the road and my reaction. "I know this is going to sound funny, but last week when I was at his house, all I could think of was introducing you to him. And when he called yesterday, I told him I was bringing someone with me that he needed to meet. I think you'll have a lot in common."

Well, this was certainly a very curious first. This time I turned in my seat to face him. "You mean you told him you were bringing your assistant?" I was really confused. "I thought this was a business errand, Ken, and what is it exactly that you think we'll have in common?"

Staring straight ahead, his left hand tapping the wheel, he answered, "What is it you always say? Wait, you'll see. I told him your name, but I didn't tell him you were my assistant."

Now he was hedging. "And it *is* about business," he went on, "but this is different, Karen. He's different, and I can't tell him that you're my assistant, because he would know I was lying." Softer now, almost to himself: "And I can never lie to him."

Now, I really did want to know. "Okay, *now* I'm asking. Who is this man you think I should know, that you think I'll have a lot in common with?"

I had been so fixated on Ken's face during our trip that I didn't realize how slowly he had been moving. I barely noticed he had slipped into a parking space and silenced the engine. Almost seamlessly, he removed the key from the ignition with his right hand while pushing the car door open with his left. With one foot out in the street, ready to exit the car, he twisted around, to look directly in my eyes. "It's Peter Hurkos, Karen," he said, lifting himself out of the car, slamming his door on my words.

"Oh my God! Peter Hurkos!" Suddenly a peaceful feeling of déjà vu, mixed with an unfamiliar case of nerves, welled up within me—as though I was visiting someone I had known all my life, but hadn't seen in many years. Though it felt like we had been driving for half an hour, in reality Ken must have been driving at a crawl, because we were in Studio City, only ten minutes from my mother's store.

Looking up to the right, I saw a beautifully landscaped house on a knoll, set back from the street. Appearing at my door, Ken offered his hand to help me out. Face to face now, we just looked at each other, silently turning to walk toward the house.

I instinctively knew this house. I intimately knew the layout of the rooms and the warm, dark woods of the furniture, the tiles in the kitchen, and the glass doors overlooking a lovely backyard. I could see it, before ever stepping foot past the front door.

Standing on the porch, I was calm on the outside and trembling on the inside. With his finger poised on the doorbell, Ken turned to look at me with a sudden softness in his eyes. "Now you understand."

The sound of bells began chiming somewhere deep within the house, as though to underscore his words. I was still nodding softly as the front door opened, and there, standing squarely in the doorway, was the world-famous psychic Peter Hurkos, a man I had heard about since I was a child.

Our smiles must have been contagious, as Peter wore one, too. He nodded as he looked past Ken, fixing directly on me. Although we had never met, when he looked into my eyes I felt as though I had known him my entire life, and the familiar kindness in his eyes said that he knew me, too.

Without a word, Peter reached past Ken, offering his hand to lead me into his home. It all seemed so natural, delicately leading me up the single, small step into rooms so familiar to my soul. I inhaled, realizing I knew the smells of this house. The subtle aroma of furniture polish and spices that went along with the larger-than-life man living there.

Ken trailed behind as Peter led me into a rectangular dining room featuring wall-to-wall glass doors overlooking a beautifully manicured backyard. The sunlit, glistening surfaces of the rich dark woods made me self-conscious about leaving fingerprints on the table.

Peter pulled a chair out, gently releasing my hand while guiding me into the seat. Ken walked around the rectangular table, taking the chair facing mine.

Leaning over my left shoulder, Peter moved in close to my face, his deeply accented voice now filling my head. "Are you comfortable? Can I get you something to drink?" His warm, mellow voice sounded like it had been aged in wood.

Covering the few steps to the kitchen, he turned, anticipating my answer: "Yes, thank you. Some ice water, please."

My eyes must have been as big as saucers when I looked across the table at Ken, and in the silent language of friends, the look between us said it all. He knew how much meeting Peter meant to me.

In that small moment Peter reappeared holding two frosty glasses. With one swift but graceful move, he brought both glasses down in place: an iced tea for Ken, and a glass of ice water for me. Before I could even utter a word of thanks, he had disappeared back into the kitchen. I took a deep breath, silently watching water drops form on the highly polished surface of the table.

With ice water in hand, Peter was back in the doorway, quickly looking back and forth between Ken's iced tea and my water. Satisfied that he had gotten everything right, he casually slid into the seat next to me. I carefully studied him as he leaned forward and took a sip from his glass before placing it on the table next to mine.

Ken and Peter leapt into conversation, as though they had just been interrupted in the middle of a sentence. They were finishing up the details about movies Peter wanted Ken to bring next, and what he wanted him to take back to storage.

I occasionally took a sip from my glass, consciously trying to place it in exactly the same wet circle on the table every time. Peter was completely oblivious about my concerns over fingerprints and water rings on the furniture; he didn't care. I watched him repeatedly pick up his glass and take a drink, putting it down wherever it landed, making an ever-widening pattern of wet rings on the table in front of us.

I just watched and listened to Ken and Peter talk, as they clearly enjoyed each other's company. Their conversation was a combination of serious business and good-natured chuckles, effortlessly weaving both elements into a single sentence. The words moved rapidly between them, bouncing from one thing to another without a single note being taken.

Though I hadn't moved and had been sitting there like a statue the entire time, a mysterious shift had taken place between them. As hard as I tried, I realized that all of a sudden I couldn't understand a thing they were saying. Sitting next to Peter, I felt like I was being let in on a secret, or was hearing a rarely spoken foreign language for the first time.

I carefully followed the changes of tone in their voices, but it became increasingly obvious that it was some kind of verbal shorthand. Over the years they had developed a language all their own. One that was clearly only meant to be spoken and understood by them, a language from their hearts that took me many years to understand.

Peter's warmth of spirit filled the room. I didn't belong, nor was I invited, to participate in their conversation. Yet in some unspoken way, Peter made me feel very welcome in his home, like he was glad I was there. His highly animated way of communicating, talking with his hands and occasionally waving in the air along with his words, provided me with an oddly familiar comfort.

I had accompanied Ken to many of his clients' homes, but this felt distinctly different. His other clients were strictly business, nothing personal. They were unfailingly nice to Ken, but it was always kept short and to the point. As expected, I was unimportant to them, so I was usually treated like a piece of furniture. I knew these people were Ken's clients, but I never felt they were his friends. Peter was definitely Ken's friend.

Their business took about an hour to complete, but never once during that time did I ever feel like a piece of furniture. Even when they mysteriously disappeared into another room to deal with something, they politely excused themselves.

Though my nervousness didn't go away, it was clear that Peter and I had a powerful connection. We knew each other before a word was ever spoken between us. It was strange, because I never get nervous, under any circumstances, so it was a little confusing to have this reaction to meeting Peter. I had to figure it out, and was happy to have a few quiet minutes to close my eyes and meditate. Sitting for less than five minutes, I cleared my mind, focusing only on this unusual situation. By the time I opened my eyes, my confusion had given way to a deep sense of peace within me, and I understood quite clearly what had triggered this unfamiliar feeling.

I laughed when I realized what it was. It was the "little girl from Los Angeles" that still lives within me. The part of me that grew up hearing stories about the incredible psychic gifts of Peter Hurkos. I was simply "starstruck"!

I was in complete awe that I was actually sitting here with Peter Hurkos, making water circles on his dining room table. The spiritual comfort between us came from a very different place. Our souls had recognized each other. We were kindred spirits, sharing the warmth of instant recognition and familiarity. This was the place where our connection lived.

Peter and Ken had what appeared to be impeccable timing. I had barely finished having my "Aha!" moment when they slipped back into their chairs. I was happy they were back.

Peter twisted his large frame sideways in his chair; he wanted to face me. His knees were little more than an inch away, with his left arm perched on the high back of his chair. His right hand casually held the dripping glass of water. He began sliding it around in the water rings, making one big wet spot on the table in front of us: his purposeful, playful way of telling me not to worry about unimportant things, and that we were one. He had a big smile on his face and mischief in his eyes. "Were we gone long enough?" he asked.

My case of nerves had vanished, and I was completely comfortable now. "Absolutely. Your timing was perfect."

His voice was soft. "I thought you might need a minute alone."

I reached for the glass in front of me and said, "Thank you. I did, but I'm fine now." I took a small sip, setting the glass down amidst the ever-spreading water rings.

Putting his hand on my arm, like old friends do, Peter said, "Can I get you some more water, Karen?"

The caring tone in his voice made me want to hug him, but instead I just turned my head and looked at him. "No, really, I'm fine."

He slowly moved his hand up my arm, as though he was reaching for the water glass I was holding. I released it, but his hand kept moving toward my wrist—and instead of picking up the glass, he gently took my hand.

I had been trying gracefully to get out of his way, but we were sitting pretty close, so my arm was practically in midair when his big hand enveloped mine. He had very subtly been leaning in closer to me since he came back into the room, and we were practically touching at this point.

I looked down at my little hand being held ever so gently by his great big hand. It was such a lovely moment. Peter brought my hand closer, suddenly fascinated by the ring I was wearing. "What is that ring? What kind of stone is it?"

Now we were both looking at my ring as I answered, "My mother had it made for me when she went to Mexico several years ago. It's a smoky topaz. I really love it."

I was looking at Peter, but he was still taken with my ring. "It's lovely. Do you wear it all the time?"

He was looking to me for an answer. I said, "Yes, it's my favorite ring. I wear it every day."

He had his other hand out now, palm up, wanting to see my ring up close. "May I see it?"

I couldn't move my hand, but answered with, "Oh, of course, let me take it off."

Peter didn't move, except to look over at Ken. "You've been awfully quiet over there," Peter said to him, suddenly realizing that I couldn't give him my ring if he didn't let go of my hand. Leaning back a little in his chair, he reluctantly let go, sliding his hand across the table in front of him.

Ken was happy that he had introduced us. "You guys were having such a good time, I didn't want to interrupt you. I had a feeling you would like each other."

That brought a quick smile from both of us. With a flourish, I slid the ring off my finger, dropping it into

Peter's hand. He said, "I would keep listening to those feelings if I were you, because I would say you were very right."

A curiously fleeting look passed between Peter and Ken, one that I didn't quite understand at the time. It wasn't exactly a smile; it felt more like another secret they shared, and I wasn't supposed to know.

Peter had become very still. Holding my ring tightly in one hand for a few minutes, he didn't move at all, silently sitting next to me with his eyes closed.

I looked over at Ken, hoping for some sort of wordless explanation. He offered none.

When Peter opened his eyes, he deftly plucked the ring out of his now-open hand and slipped it on the tip of his right index finger. Carefully positioning the ring on his finger, and finally satisfied that it was where he wanted it, he brought it up to his face for a closer look.

Without a word, he placed his left hand on my wrist, lifting my arm up with him, as he stood straight up from his chair. Looking down at me, and with a suddenly merry tone in his voice, he said, "It needs cleaning, Karen. Come in the kitchen with me, and we will clean your ring together."

What a funny sight this must have been. There I was, with my arm kind of hanging in the air, as Peter stood next to me, wearing my ring on his right index finger.

I looked over at Ken, but he was looking up at Peter when he finally spoke. "Go on, Karen. Peter is very good at cleaning jewelry."

I caught a glimpse of that look, passing between them again.

Peter was still holding my wrist as I stood up, and he gently led me between the chairs, moving me into the kitchen and toward the sink. Turning me by my shoulders so we were facing each other, he let my hand fall for a moment to remove my ring from his finger. Without uttering a word he raised my left hand and positioned the ring where he wanted it now, on my left index finger.

Turning me around to face the sink, he stood behind me, carefully guiding my arms over the edge, so that my hands hung out into the center of the sink. Peter reached past me to turn the water on. I watched his fingers wiggle under the tap, as he tested the water temperature, staying like that until the water got hot enough. Since he hadn't said a word since we entered the kitchen, I teased him, "Do you clean everyone's rings, Peter?"

His voice was gentle and kind. "No, but I wanted to clean yours. It's special to you, and should be kept beautiful."

Without another word, he took a toothbrush from the windowsill, reaching out with his other hand and removing a small dish from the side of the sink. Placing the brush in my right hand and the small dish in my left, he placed his hands directly over mine.

Methodically, Peter guided our hands under the faucet—first wetting the brush, then moving it over to the substance in the dish. He guided my right hand in circles, swirling the wet bristles around the top of the cleaning material, repeating this action several times until he was satisfied with the way the brush looked.

He placed the dish back in its place, ready to clean my ring. With the precision of a chemist, with only Peter knowing the magic formula, we repeatedly brushed all sides of the stone. Very gently he removed the ring from my fingertip, turning it upside down. Once this was done, we carefully applied Peter's jewelry cleaning formula to the underside of the stone, and finally to the gold mounting.

Happy with the procedure, we thoroughly rinsed out the brush, rinsed off my ring, and turned off the faucets. Peter took the ring from my hands, stepping back to grab a towel.

I turned to face him, but he was focused intently on my ring. "Well, how does it look, Doctor Peter?"

While carefully drying every surface, he periodically held it up to the light coming in the kitchen window to check for water spots. Finally happy with the results, he gently took both of my hands in one of his, sliding the ring back where it belonged, slightly tightening his grip on my hands.

His whole energy changed as he spoke, saying what he had been wanting to say since opening the front door, and it wasn't about my ring. "Karen, I know you are going through a difficult time right now, but everything is going to be all right. I promise. Please, don't ever doubt, and don't worry. Please, don't look back. You must keep going."

He had barely finished his words when I burst into tears and couldn't stop. Putting his arms around me, he continued in the softest, most gentle voice. "Don't worry, Karen, I promise. Everything will be all right. Just keep going, because you are doing what you are *supposed* to be doing, and you *should* never, and *must* never, question it."

We must have stood there for ten minutes, me sobbing and Peter comforting me.

If it had been anyone but Peter, I would have been deeply embarrassed. But he knew me, and he knew how I felt. He understood how difficult finding my way had been. Without a word, he knew how painfully sensitive I was, and that everything my clients felt, I felt deeply as well. He knew exactly what I had been going through.

Without my ever asking, Peter had delivered the answer I had been asking God to provide for years, and he knew it. He also knew that the few sentences he uttered to me in his kitchen that day would profoundly change my life forever.

Sobbing in Peter's comforting hug, the weight I had carried in my soul since childhood was lifted. For many years I had asked God for clarity about my gift. Peter saw that in me, and knew that I was ready to hear it.

I couldn't stop sobbing, but my tears were no longer tears of pain. Now they were tears of joy. They signaled the deep and lasting peace that had finally found a home in my heart.

Peter led me to the sink, so I could wash my face with cool water. He placed his hands on my shoulders, tipping my chin upward to look in my eyes. "I am glad you came today, Karen. You needed to hear this, and now you will be fine."

Stepping back into the dining room, I thought I would have to explain my hysterical crying in the kitchen to Ken, but he never said a word about it. Not then, or ever.

That magical day of tears and peace was the beginning of a lifelong friendship between Peter and me, and I hold many precious memories in my heart for this wonderful man. Every time I pass a Du-par's Restaurant, I think of his lovely laugh, and the kindness in his beautiful heart, and I am forever grateful that he was one of the angels in my life, sent to calm the soul of a prayerful sixteen-year-old, long searching for an answer.

Those looks between Peter and Ken, the ones I didn't understand at the time, after that day so many years ago, I finally understand what they meant. I realized that though I may never have been able to translate their verbal shorthand, I had spoken their "secret" language of the heart all along.

4

The Socialite

Through this particular reading for a socialite I learned a painful truth about the old saying "You can't judge a book by its cover." After her reading with me, I realized that, as human beings, we will instill qualities in people they may never possess. I also learned the difference between what we wish for a person to be, and who they truly are. After meeting the socialite, I never looked at people through quite the same eyes again.

In early September 1979 I flew to Texas to be interviewed for a front-page article in a major newspaper. The three-hour interview was done rather casually over dinner at a steakhouse in Houston with the reporter and her husband.

The reporter was the friend of a very prominent architect and a longtime client of mine. She had been told about me and the outcome of his readings with me, both personal and business readings that took place several times over the course of a couple of years.

In 1979 in Texas, a psychic from California was an oddity altogether. Writing a story about a psychic at all I thought was pretty brave, and I wondered if the newspaper would even print the story. The reporter was highly respected, and the editor not only said yes but also put the story on the front page of the Lifestyle section of their Sunday edition.

The response was overwhelming.

One day, in the midst of the bazillion readings generated from the article, I answered the door to find a stunningly beautiful, dark-haired lady of about forty years old. She was my next appointment. I showed her into the living room and had her sign my client book, while I removed the tape she presented and slipped it into my tape recorder.

Everything about this beautiful woman appeared to have a designer label on it. Her face was Charles of the Ritz; her blouse was Gucci; her skirt was Escada; and her dainty feet were encased in shoes by my favorite shoe designer, Stuart Weitzman.

She had a diamond on her hand and one in each ear, as big as my eyes. Her husband owned several insurance agencies throughout Texas. The prior Christmas he had presented her with a Rolls Royce convertible, laden with more gifts covering the back seat.

She had beautiful sons who were truly exceptional in every way. One was fair in coloring and light-eyed; the other, dark-haired and brown-eyed. They were handsome boys and perfect students who achieved straight As across the board at private school. They excelled at playing lacrosse, rowing, and seemingly every other thing they did.

This woman appeared to have a truly perfect marriage, perfect children, and a seemingly perfect life.

As I moved further into her reading, however, stepping past her "perfect" life, a man who was clearly not her husband appeared to me in her reading. I started describing this man to her: "I see another man around you. He is about 5'11", slim, with beautiful salt-and-pepper hair. He sounds American, but is definitely foreign-born, with olive skin, more Mediterranean in coloring."

I paused for a moment. "This comes as a very *intimate* type of relationship. Do you know who this gentleman is?"

She had become slightly uncomfortable, looking down at her hands clasped tightly in her lap. She demurely responded in her softest Texas drawl, "Uh-huh," drawing out each syllable.

She continued staring at her hands, without so much as a glance when I spoke. "There appears to be a rather upsetting situation involving this gentleman right now. Do you understand what I mean?"

Murmuring again: "Uh-huh."

This time I measured my words. "This is a deeply spiritual man, a man with deep religious convictions and a *very* strong relationship with God. This appears to be a very complicated relationship with you. Do you know who I'm talking about?"

She finally looked at me with those big brown eyes, and was practically purring "Uh-huh."

I finally asked, "Who is he, dear?"

Without missing a beat, she kept looking directly at me as she spoke. "Umm, it's my priest."

Taking a deep breath, I found myself sputtering, "No, no, dear…this couldn't be your priest. I mean this looks like a *very* complicated…*very intimate* relationship, one that is causing him a great deal of pain."

I took a deep breath, patiently asking again, "Now do you know who this is?"

Suddenly, the purring stopped, along with her practiced softness, as she practically snapped at me, "Yes, it's my priest."

I thought that I must not be making myself clear. "No, no, this couldn't be your priest, dear. I mean, it can't be, because what I am looking at is *definitely* a sexual relationship."

I am certain she thought that I must be deaf. Defiantly leaning forward, the edge even sharper in her voice now, she said, "Uh-huh, it's my priest."

I was in my twenties at this time, and still living under some silly illusion that a priest would never, ever have an affair. Let alone with a married woman.

Absolutely astonished, I quietly asked, "You're having sex with your priest?"

Naively, I kept on insisting that it couldn't be him. It simply couldn't be. Though in my bones I knew it was true. I could see him as clear as a bell in her reading, and he came to me as a devoutly religious man. I just didn't want to believe it.

Just to clarify it for myself, I asked another question. "If you are having sex with your priest, then why does this feel like he's trying to pull away and end this relationship?"

She was pouting now. "Because he *does* want to end it! You see, he, my husband, and I have been having three-ways, and *he* wants to stop!"

I was in utter disbelief, not that she ever bothered to notice, and I could barely get my next questions out. "You're having three-ways with your priest? And, *you're* upset that he wants to end this? And, why exactly are you upset?"

If she could have stomped her foot, I think she certainly would have. With great defiance, sniping at me like I was just an idiot and couldn't possibly understand, she blurted out, "Because we *like* it!"

I sat back in my chair for a moment just looking at her. I was speechless, and had to think, if only for a moment.

This absolutely elegant woman looked as though she had stepped off the page of a magazine. Everything about her was simply stunning. She had jet-black hair, big brown eyes, and porcelain skin. I finally got it. She was perfect and clearly living in her own perfect little world.

I excused myself for a moment as I turned off the tape recorder, walking into the kitchen to pour myself a big cup of coffee. I felt like I had just been kicked in the stomach, and could barely breathe. I was in the kitchen about three minutes, just long enough to center myself again.

I came back, sat down, and turned the tape recorder on, with the stark realization that she simply didn't get it. She couldn't "see" what I saw.

Softly, I continued. "I understand that you like this, and I can hear the frustration in your voice, but this man took a vow of celibacy in his dedication to God. Can you not see that he has profound regrets about his actions, and that he can no longer live with this duplicity in his life?"

Defiantly, and practically shouting, she glared at me and said, "But, I don't *want* him to stop!"

Her reaction was so painful for me.

This beautiful woman, with an amazing life, was having three-ways with her priest. She couldn't even remotely understand why he wanted to go back to the church.

I was trying to reach her heart. I wanted to help her find the most unselfish part of herself. Reaching over, I touched her hand, tenderly asking, "Do you care about this man?"

She hung her head, and with tears in her eyes, softly replied, "Uh-huh."

I knew that whatever caring meant to her, she truly did. "If you truly care about him, then you must step back from your feelings and allow him to go back to the life he chose. Can't you see that this is torturing him, that this has created great conflict in his soul? I don't believe that you want to cause him any more pain. Do you?"

Hesitantly, but calmer, she said, "No, I don't want him to be in pain."

Continuing, I said, "Then you must let him go."

Drying her tears and thinking more clearly now, she said, "I never looked at it that way, Karen."

I had found the way to her heart. "I want you to promise me that you will let him go back to the church."

It was funny how quickly she appeared to resolve the issue regarding her priest, or so it seemed, but she wasn't done. Her next question just made me laugh inside.

She asked me if she would ever find anyone else to have three-ways with. I assured her that she would and that she would find other venues, outside of the church, to find that next person.

At the end of the reading, she told me that she felt so much better, because now she understood why he didn't want to continue. As long as she was sure they would find someone else to play with, she was fine.

When she left, I walked into the bathroom, looked at myself in the mirror, and said, "Oh, grow up, Karen."

What profound realizations this reading had brought for me.

Here was this lovely man who clearly loved God, loved being a priest, loved the church, and yet, he was human. He had fallen from grace, and was suffering terribly over his transgressions.

She was a woman who had everything a person could ask for in life. She had a loving husband who spoiled her, wonderful children, a beautiful home, her health, and the health of her family. Yet she was absolutely incapable of seeing past her own selfish needs.

These were great lessons.

I learned that all people, whether devoutly religious or not, truly are only human.

Only God is perfect.

It was the child in me that was so shocked. The part of me that grew up naively believing that priests, rabbis, and all holy men were different, that they were above all earthly temptations.

This woman and her husband had been having sex with their priest, without the slightest hint of conscience about the consequences. The only part of it she could begin to understand was that it was causing him great pain, great spiritual pain.

She said that she never thought about it that way, and all I wondered was, how she could not?

He had been dedicated to God's work as a priest for twenty-five years, and had fallen. His shame was unbearable. It was so clear to me that he was having an impossible time reconciling his spiritual duties and his relationship with God with his all-too-human desires of the flesh.

I felt terribly sad for him, because these were such personal issues. They were between him and God, and he had broken his promise with God. Now he would live with the consequences of his actions for the rest of his life.

She said her husband had taken pictures of them, and all I could think about was how difficult it was for the priest to realize he was human.

I know that some people have no conscience, but I knew that *this* man would spend the rest of his days trying to make it up to God.

It delivered a crystal-clear message for me that it was tough being human.

This particular reading had a profound effect on my life. I knew in my heart that the priest's actions didn't change his vow to God. I realized that his desire for intimacy with another person truly is a part of being human.

I saw with stark clarity the price he was paying, and would continue to pay, for his behavior. It is emotionally and spiritually deeper, and more profoundly painful, for someone who has a powerful relationship with God.

Throughout my life I have repeatedly been exposed to a disturbing yet profound experience and, sadly, one that we all share. It is that people seldom are who they represent themselves to be. Sometimes there is so much more to them than meets the eye, and of course there are times when we instill in people qualities they do not possess, only to be surprised and disappointed by their lack.

As human beings we carry the unspoken expectation of how people are *supposed* to behave, but I have learned that our expectations will only be as lenient, or as rigid, as our frame of reference.

Human nature is born with a hunger, a natural curiosity to seek out what is denied. I am less naïve now, and know that simply because a person presents themselves to be religious, their relationship with God doesn't mean they have lost their hunger.

This particular reading in Texas was the first of many readings connected to religion, with many priests and nuns being drawn to me for readings over the years. It saddens me to see how many of them live with painfully deep conflict, in their desire to serve God. They have made commitments and taken vows, yet live with the constant uncertainty of being human.

When counseling people in service to God, my desire is to help them find peace within their soul—to help them reconcile two seemingly disparate elements, those of spirituality and human desire, which live within us all.

5

The Librarian

Although I have read for thousands of people over the years and all over the world, this story is, by far, the saddest reading I have ever given. This reading taught me about the paralyzing consequences of fear, and how powerful free will can truly be. All we have to do is make a choice to confront the fear of change that takes up residence in our mind. I learned that on any given day, we can heal our pain and change our circumstances by putting forth even the slightest effort. It only takes a moment to make that decision, and by taking even a baby step forward, we can change our life.

Many people have touched my life in some way, but few as deeply as a lady I met one cloudy winter day in New York City.

I was blessed with a truly wonderful mother. She was born in Brooklyn and had a New Yorker's sensibility. Because of her, I carry within my heart a deep and special love for everything about New York.

During a highly active bicoastal period in my life, spanning almost twenty years, I can honestly say that I never experienced a single moment of boredom in the Big Apple. Just walking down the street there is an experience.

Having lived in some of the most beautiful cities in the world, I still feel that there is simply no place that feels anything like New York City. It vibrates with a life and energy all its own, and without a doubt remains one of the most magical, exhilarating, passionate, and diverse cities in the world.

For several years my home in Manhattan was a suite at the Mayflower Hotel. It was a lovely older hotel across from Central Park, providing a perfect location for me and easy access for my clients.

I was practically around the corner from ABC Television, the studio where I often shot *The Morning Show* with Regis Philbin, and a short taxi ride from ABC Radio, where I had become a frequent guest on a variety of call-in shows.

Over the years, I have had the opportunity to meet with people from every possible walk of life: from garbage collectors to aristocrats, cat groomers to movie stars, and everyone in between. One thing I know with certainty is that every single human being has a purpose in this world, and contrary to popular belief, everybody's life is different.

I have often wondered how any of us survive our childhoods. When emotional traumas are inflicted on the young, intentionally or not, those experiences can leave scars that are carried well into adulthood, unconsciously impacting every part of a person's life.

We all have them. Some people wear them on the outside, by making themselves emotionally and/or physically unavailable. They unconsciously erect a protective shell of some kind, to keep people away.

For others it manifests as a deeply profound emotional and spiritual pain that continues to paralyze their lives at every turn.

There have been a few clients over the years whose scars have left me with an indelible sadness that will forever make my soul weep.

Marta Alberts was one of those people.

It was late in the afternoon when Marta lightly knocked on my door. Possessing a soft, old-fashioned energy, she seemed to carry quiet within her very being.

A tentative quality guided her steps to my sofa, and in some unconscious way she reminded me of my grandmother. It wasn't a literal physical resemblance, but more in the way she carried herself, feeling much older than her years.

Marta was somewhere in her mid-fifties. She was thickly built, wearing a dark, grayish-brown dress below the knee, with an embroidered Peter Pan collar and a thin belt fashioned from the same fabric. She wore black, functional shoes with sturdy heels that laced up the front. She wore no jewelry except a small, oval-faced silver watch with barely readable numbers and a slim, flexible band.

She wore no makeup—not mascara, not lipstick, nothing. Her hair was a mousy brown with an occasional wild gray hair, pulled back in a home-style bun. She had a soft, full face and beautiful skin, with large, expressive hazel eyes, natural eyebrows, an inherited jowl, and a body that was more round than svelte. There was something old-fashioned yet very beautiful about her to me, and something incredibly sad.

Smiling, I held my client sign-in book and one of my business cards out to her. "Did you bring a tape?" I asked her.

Taking the open book and card from my hands, she responded in an expectedly soft voice, "No, I don't think I'll need one."

Cheerily, I said, "Well, I hope you have a good memory, because I cover a lot of ground."

She finished signing my book, quietly closing it as she held it out for me to take. Crossing her legs at the ankles, she finally looked directly at me. "So, how do we do this?"

When our eyes met, the air in the room suddenly became thick. The cool crispness was replaced with an unexplainable heaviness.

Taking the book, I looked away to place it on the coffee table, my eyes suddenly stinging with tears. I took a breath, grabbed a Kleenex to dry my unexpected tears, and mumbled something about allergies. Excusing myself for a minute, I slipped into the bathroom, certain she wouldn't understand the overwhelming sadness I was feeling at that moment any better than I did.

I came out of the bathroom with a couple of Kleenex gripped firmly in my hand. Settling in my chair across from Marta, I sputtered out an excuse. "Sorry about that, the tears just seemed to leap out of my eyes. It must be an allergy attack. Now, if you have something you have worn for a year or more, like a ring, watch, or keys, we'll get started."

Quietly she reached into her purse, extracting her keys. Holding them in her hand, she placed her hands in her lap, making no move to give the keys to me. More directly this time, she repeated her original question: "So, how do we do this?"

I had been so flustered by the sudden wave of tears that it took me a minute to respond, "Oh, yes, I'm sorry, you did ask me that. Well, I hold your keys for a minute. I do a quiet little meditation, and then I start your reading."

That wasn't detailed enough for her. "Do you need any information from me? Like my date of birth or anything?"

I guess she expected something else. Many readers light candles and incense, or want you to take off your shoes. They might request that you not cross your arms or legs during the reading, as it might block the energy. They may have a crystal they hold, or want you to hold, or they want your birth information. I don't do any of those things.

I say a silent meditation that takes about one minute, hand back whatever object the person has given me, turn on the tape recorder if they have brought a tape, and start talking. Every reader has rituals. Silently reciting a meditation prayer that I wrote many years ago is my *only* ritual.

I held my hand out for the keys. "No, just your keys, please. Hold on for a second and you'll see."

Marta watched me cautiously as she placed her keys in my open hand. Closing my eyes, my hand around the keys, I silently recited my meditation prayer.

There is an order to the importance of issues in every reading. It is not my decision, nor do I randomly choose where to start. The order always shows itself during my meditation, when I step into the energy for the person and begin.

If my client has brought pictures of anyone they want to know about, or documents, contracts, or business cards, I place them in front of me on the table before my meditation or before starting the client's reading.

Every reader works differently; for me, giving a reading is like "being there." It is as though I step "into the client's life" for the duration of the reading, and am with them in the experience. I seldom look at or focus on the pictures and other things, until I have thoroughly dealt with the most important issues first. When I am finished with those, I proceed to the photos, contracts, business cards, or the like.

Occasionally, clients will ask if they can, or should, bring a list of questions. I tell them to go ahead and make the list, but to please keep it in their pocket or purse until

I am finished. If I haven't answered all of the questions on their list, I will gladly answer them when I am done. I have found that I have usually answered everything, and then some, on the list.

Marta brought no photos, no documents, no contracts, no business cards, and no list. Just Marta.

An enveloping sadness came over me during my meditation for Marta's reading. In one small, synchronized movement, I opened my eyes while pouring the keys into her outstretched palm. "What a lovely home you have; it feels like you have lived there all your life." I walked through the rooms of her home in my mind, describing in detail what I saw.

Carefully choosing my words, I continued. "You have had so much loss. I keep looking at a bedroom in your home, set up like a hospital room, but I see several different people in the same bed, but at different times."

She was very still, tightly clutching the keys in her hands, clasped rigidly together in her lap. Marta barely murmured, "Yes, that's right. It's my family home, and it's the only place I've ever lived, and yes, you're right about the bedroom, too."

I couldn't look into her eyes or I would have burst into tears. I shifted my gaze to focus on the gray New York sky hovering outside the window, the weather seeming to reflect the emotion I felt for this lovely woman. "You have been the caregiver: not just for them, but for everyone in your family. I see an older woman, and then a man. They feel like your mother and father."

In barely a whisper, Marta confirmed my words. "Yes, they were both in that room."

I could hardly get the words out as water filled my eyes. "They were sick, and then left, back to back," I said, turning to look at her as the first tears tumbled down my cheeks. "You took care of them all by yourself. I don't see any brothers or sisters, no other family to help you. Just you."

Her voice was barely audible now, as tears began spilling from her eyes. "I was an only child, so there was no one to help me."

Realizing the sadness had finally overtaken both of us, I reached for a box of Kleenex on the table, holding it up between us. Now I understood what I had been feeling for her, and why.

I knew at that moment that the weeping between us wasn't going to stop until I finished her reading. "I see that you lost both of your parents within a very short period of time, and I am looking at another elderly man in that bed now. He feels like your uncle."

She was weeping quietly, "Yes, he is dying now, too."

The tears kept flowing as our tissues piled up in the trash. "It's almost over, sweetheart, and you know he is getting ready to leave. Oh, I'm so sorry, Marta. This has been going on for so many years: the illness, the loss, and then the cycle feels like it has repeated over and over again, and now with your uncle."

Her words seemed to come from someplace far away, "Yes, it has been going on for a very long time, and I know it won't be much longer for my uncle. I will miss him terribly, because he's the last one left in my family."

I needed to look at another area of Marta's life or I was going to drown in my tears. "I want to talk to you about your job now. Do you work around a lot of books? I keep seeing you surrounded by books." Lowering my voice, I said, "I want to whisper when I talk about your job. It feels so quiet there. Are you a librarian?"

Sweetly now: "Yes, well, actually I'm a medical librarian, and it is very quiet there."

I saw the light in Marta's eyes as I spoke. "Well, you know you can stay there as long as you want. I see that they're modernizing the facility, so there will be some new procedures you'll be required to learn, but aside from those little issues, you definitely have security there. Wow! You've been there a long time, and they just love you."

Marta was beaming with pride. "Yes, I've been there over thirty years. It's the only job I've ever known, and they are *such* nice people to work with. After all this time, they're almost like my family."

I moved forward. "I know you don't travel much, but do you ever get away? Even for a weekend?"

Marta looked surprised. "Oh, I've never been out of New York! I've gone between Brooklyn and the city my whole life. I've never traveled anywhere, Karen."

I was overwhelmed by the incredibly small world Marta lived in, and had lived in her entire life. "Not even for a weekend? Haven't you ever wanted to travel?"

She was composed now. "I wanted to travel once, but then I got my job, and who would take care of my family if I went away somewhere?"

The sadness I had fought off earlier loomed in front of me once again. I could only tell her what I saw. "I don't see a husband or boyfriend here either, Marta. You've never been married." It was a statement of fact, not a question.

Pain underlined her every word. "No … no husband. I've never been married, but you knew that, Karen. I've never even had a boyfriend."

I thought the grief in my heart for the tragedy of this beautiful woman's life was going to completely overtake me. I could barely speak. Fighting the onslaught of tears was simply useless, as I was certain I was drowning. Once again I was diving into the box of Kleenex, only this time I was grabbing them by the handful.

Marta's lonely, empty world of duty and denial threatened to swallow me whole.

There were no more tears from Marta. She looked at me with quiet concern in her eyes. "Are you okay, Karen?"

My body shook, wracked by gut-wrenching sobs, as I buried my face in a wad of Kleenex, trying to choke out my anguished words. "Why did you come to see me? I can't tell you that anything is going to change. I can't make something up."

She was quiet for several minutes, her steady gaze watching as my body shook with pain and grief, for her.

When she finally spoke, her words were soft and filled with resignation. "I just wanted confirmation, and I knew *you* would tell me the truth. I knew *you* wouldn't lie to me. I am sorry this is so painful for you, but this is my life."

Realizing how calm she was, and how completely resigned to her life she truly was, began to quiet my grief. "Oh, Marta, I wish I could change something for you, but I can't. You were a great gift to your family, do you know that?"

A faint smile crossed her lips. "Yes, and they were wonderful parents. They were *my* gift." In a way I couldn't begin to understand, she felt more peaceful. "Thank you for this," she said.

I was incredulous. "This what? You are thanking me for telling you this is your life, and nothing is ever going to change?"

Marta's smile brought an abrupt end to my tears. Clearly we looked at her reading through very different eyes. "Yes, I know this is my life, Karen. I only wanted confirmation, and that is what you gave me. I knew that my life was never going to change, and I got exactly what I came for, so yes, thank you."

We talked for a few minutes without tears, before she went home to take care of her uncle. Marta's life remained exactly as it had been an hour and a half earlier. She was content and peaceful with her reading.

I, however, had been deeply affected, and forever changed by the circumstances of her life and by what I had experienced in her reading. The sadness she left me with never really went away. Even now, as I write her story, I cry when I think about the tiny world she inhabited, for almost sixty years.

This beautiful woman had never traveled more than five miles from her home, and never would. The same home she had been brought home to as a newborn was the only one she had known, and would ever know. She had nursed both her mother and father for many years until their deaths, and was now taking care of her terminally ill uncle.

This was her life.

All of the circumstances in Marta's life saddened me. I wished for so much more for her. I wished for her a bigger, fuller, emotionally fulfilled life, but that was not the destiny she had chosen. This was.

There was one tragic reality of Marta's life that has impacted me deeply since the day I met her. One I weep over, still.

This warm, smart, kind, beautiful woman had never known any other love except parental love. No one had ever so much as held her hand. She had never loved or been loved, and had never experienced so much as the passion of a lover's kiss. I knew with great certainty that Marta had never known the joy of being in love, nor would it ever be a part of her life.

Marta continues to teach me about the choices we make in life. She repeatedly made choices over the years that further served to compact her life, and always consciously chose the safety of certainty.

Surely there are many different, less certain roads along life's journey, yet when no emotional risk is ever taken, and certainty becomes the only choice ever made, we greatly diminish our lives.

By never stepping outside of what is comfortable and familiar, we miss experiencing the immeasurable richness and growth that love can bring into our lives.

When I think about Marta, I think about the fear she clasped so closely to her chest, and her emotionally paralyzing fear of change. Her fear had become the foundation and motivation in her life, enabling her to relinquish total control of her life to circumstance.

Her fear dictated her fate. Marta chose to turn the part of her life as caregiver of her family into 100 percent of her life. My sadness was in knowing she had quite consciously closed off all other experiences, and always would. There was no risk. She continually used fear to isolate herself, never allowing room for anyone to help her with anything.

She consciously never allowed herself a personal moment to feel joy, and, for me, the greatest tragedy of all was that she had spent a lifetime denying herself love.

I pray in some small way that I helped her find peace. I bless her every day for allowing me in. By showing me her sadness, by experiencing her paralyzing fear of love, I learned from Marta how truly empty life is without it.

The Fireman's Wife

I met Sila Albin during a particularly hectic but happy period of my life in New York. I was doing a lot of media at this time, making repeated appearances on ABC Talk Radio and as a frequent guest on *The Morning Show* with the wonderful Regis Philbin.

I was also heavily booked with readings, and though I normally set appointments with clients myself, during this very busy period I hired a secretary.

Carla's duties were to set up my appointments, return phone calls, and confirm meetings for me. I was very grateful to have her taking care of these important parts of my day, as it allowed me more time to actually give readings.

Carla worked for me consistently for a couple of years, and I liked her. She was pleasant on the phone, and she was nice to my clients and considerate of their schedules and mine when setting appointments. These are human traits that should be a normal part of life under any circumstances, but are often forgotten when people get busy. Carla knew they were important to me, and they came easily to her, so we got along just fine.

She liked working with me, and she liked having the opportunity to meet people from every walk of life who came to me for readings.

For several months she had been dealing with a recurring medical issue that I felt needed to be taken care of as soon as possible.

As we all know, our health needs to be tended to. Sometimes we can put off or delay taking care of ourselves, but when our bodies demand attention, it doesn't matter what else is going on or how busy we are. Health becomes the priority.

With every passing week, I became more concerned about Carla's health than she was, and kept urging her to take some time off to get her health back. Since she would not willingly take care of herself, I had to force her to go to the doctor by taking away her alternatives and leaving her with no other choice. Reluctantly, off to the doctor she was lovingly forced to go, along with several weeks of recuperative bed rest.

Carla's expected departure forced me to dust off my old work-related juggling skills. I welcomed the opportunity to once again set my daily schedule, organize meetings, confirm appointments, and then give the readings.

Watching me manage everything on that first day must have been pretty comical, but by the time Sila called for an appointment, my juggling skills were in good form.

I liked Sila immediately. I knew when I heard her voice that I would be happy to have this warm, loving woman in my home, and when I actually met her in person I was glad she was there. She carried the same warm energy in person that she had conveyed on the phone.

Her appointment was set for late in the day. When I opened the door, I found a full-figured, gray-haired, makeup-free, sparkly eyed woman in her late fifties. She embodied a little bit of the earth mother quality, wearing her confidence as a woman like a comfortable pair of shoes.

Sila was a rare and beautiful creature because she was a truly happy, deeply fulfilled woman. She had been married for over thirty years to a man she not only still loved but also liked as a human being. They had built a wonderful life together.

They had raised a loving son and daughter, now grown up and with identities of their own, and were longtime members of the large family of heroes within the fire department. They were salt-of-the-earth people who had succeeded in life, especially when it came to the things that truly matter.

I went into her reading covering all of the pertinent areas of her life: the recent marriage of one of her children, extended family concerns, financial matters, and finally the big issue—her husband's retirement from the fire department after over thirty years. This was a major transition point for both of them, and they were looking forward to making some big plans.

I began this part of her reading by addressing the underlying emotional issues impacting both of them: the joy, the anticipation, and the unspoken fears they both carried.

Their entire lives had revolved around her husband's life as a firefighter. For over thirty years, her flexibility with the craziness of his work schedule, accompanied by the high physical and emotional demands of the job, were all they had ever known.

This was the beginning of a new life, and they were sorting through plans for their future. I repeated an ongoing conversation I heard in the reading; it was between Sila and her husband, about selling their home and moving to Florida. I told her I saw no real substance, or commitment, to either selling or moving, and didn't see either of those things becoming a reality any time in the near future.

She was more surprised that I highlighted their exact concerns about the house and Florida, quoting their conversation verbatim, than about the fact that they weren't moving.

She jokingly told me they'd had that exact conversation often, but she couldn't recall my having ever been in their dining room on any of the occasions they had discussed it.

I laughed and said, "Well, I don't remember being in your dining room either, but I do know you will eventually sell your home and move. You won't do either for quite a while though, and I never see you living in Florida."

As I moved forward in her reading, my feelings shifted; there was real substance connected to the next issue about a trip. I saw a big trip unfolding, one they had been tentatively planning for a very long time.

It looked like a conversation that had been going on between them for years and had always been set for some vague date in the future, when her husband retired. It was his dream vacation, a lifelong dream, and in the reading it looked like Italy.

No longer surprised, Sila confirmed that yes, indeed, they had often daydreamed about her husband's desire to take a long, romantic trip to Italy. One they could take without restrictions of time or money, just the two of them.

As his retirement loomed, Italy became a daily topic and the centerpiece of their initial plans. I told her they were definitely going, because I saw them there for an entire month, and it felt like the upcoming July.

Once again my feelings were correct, and I urged her to act immediately. To please go home and make definitive plans for the entire month of July.

This was a very difficult topic for me to talk about as I felt a great urgency surrounding this trip, yet I couldn't tell her why. I had the strongest desire to hand her the phone and tell her to make the reservations right now, not to put it off for one more moment; they had waited long enough.

She casually talked about them needing to take care of things around the house before they committed to this trip.

Without alarming her, I told her those things would still be there when they returned. Everything could be taken care of when they got back.

I knew that Italy couldn't wait, and pointed out how hard they had worked to get to this place in their lives, to finally have the freedom to fulfill her husband's dream.

As though she was thinking out loud, she responded to my prodding. "I know you're right, Karen. This has been going on for such a long time; it used to be just an occasional conversation, but now he talks about going to Italy every day."

She became wistful as she continued. "We have been so lucky, and our life has been so full. It's funny, you know, I don't think we ever really believed this day would come. This trip you're talking about has been Jerry's fantasy since the day we got married, but actually going has always seemed so far away. You're right. We should stop putting it off, and just go."

I wasn't really relieved, because I knew I couldn't change what I saw, but I was grateful that she had at least, sort of, agreed to go. "Yes, you should, because that time is no longer far away. It's now, and Sila, please, I want you to promise me that you will make the reservations for the entire month of July. This is your once-in-a-lifetime trip, so please promise me that you will take a thousand pictures, do everything you and Jerry have talked about for thirty years, and let yourselves enjoy every minute of just being there together."

I finished her reading, walked her to the door, and gave her a big hug. I took a step back, feeling the need to remind her one last time, "Promise me you'll go in July and not put it off. Will you let me know?"

A soft smile played around her mouth, but her eyes still held uncertainty, and without an ounce of conviction she told me, "I promise, and yes, I'll let you know what happens."

A rush of sadness filled my heart as I closed the door. Now all I could do was hope she didn't put the practical need for new siding above her husband's dream trip to Italy.

Sila's reading crossed my mind several times in the ensuing days. My schedule was filled with a whirlwind of readings, radio shows, and an occasional business dinner.

One afternoon the phone rang between readings, with Sila's usually warm voice on the other end, now sounding very worried. "Karen? It's Sila. I'm sorry to bother you, but I am very confused."

I didn't like how she sounded. "No problem, Sila, what's the matter? You sound upset."

She was so upset that it came out in a rush: "Well, umm, you know I've been on this kind of spiritual thing lately, remember we talked about it in my reading? Well, yesterday I went to an astrologer, and I don't know if you remember us talking about the trip to Italy, but she told me not to take the trip in July. She told me to wait and make the reservations so we would leave on September ninth! I am so confused, because you were so sure. Now I don't know what to do!"

My heart filled with a terrible yet familiar sadness. I had to make sure she understood my urgency without just blurting it out. I started, "Sila, I don't know why the astrologer told you to wait until September ninth, but how do I say this to you?"

Emphasizing every word, I continued, "Sila, I am *begging* you not to wait. I am *begging* you to make the reservations and leave the first of July, and stay the entire month. I am *begging* you to take a thousand pictures on this trip and commit every moment to memory. I am *begging* you not to wait. Do you hear me?"

Now she heard me, the fear in her voice evident. "I hear you, Karen, but what will happen if we wait until September ninth to leave? Why are you so adamant about July?"

The sadness inside me swelled as I spoke. "Because if you don't go in July, you will never make this trip."

Panic filled her voice. "What do you mean we'll never take this trip? I thought you said we were definitely going? That you saw us there?"

I took a deep breath. "If you wait to go in September, you will never take this trip. I saw you and Jerry in Italy in July, *not* September. I begged you to make the reservations for July. If you wait until September ninth to leave, Jerry will never make this trip, Sila. He won't be here."

She was beside herself, now edging toward hysteria, and trying to make sense of what I had just said. "What are you saying? What do you mean he won't be here? Where is he going?"

I wanted to put my arms around her and just cry, but I couldn't. There was no easy way to tell this lovely woman that she was going to be widowed in September.

She had left me no other choice. "Sila, if you don't make this trip in July, Jerry will not be here to take it. He will not be alive to make the trip on September ninth. Now, do you understand why I was so adamant about July? Why I never saw you moving to Florida? Why the repairs on the house can wait?"

Hysteria crept into her voice. "Now what am I supposed to do? Are you sure?"

I could feel her fear. "I am more than sure. I knew it when you were here for your reading, but you were not supposed to be told. The astrologer has left me no choice, so I am asking you again. *Please* take the trip in July with Jerry and stay for the entire month; do everything he wants to do; go everywhere he wants to go; and as I asked you before, please take a thousand pictures, committing every moment of this trip to memory. If you don't take this trip in July, you will never take this trip that your husband has dreamt of for over thirty years. Take the trip in July, and call me when you come home. If Jerry is still alive on the afternoon of September tenth, Sila, please come after me. I want you to enjoy every moment with him, and call me on the tenth of September. I am deeply sorry about your loss, believe me, more than you could ever know. Please, go on the trip in July."

She was very upset, but I knew she finally understood my urgency surrounding the trip. "Why didn't you tell me during my reading? How could you not tell me? Maybe I can change it."

Knowing she couldn't understand my position, I tried to help her. "I didn't tell you because you weren't supposed to know, and it is not my decision. This is in God's hands. If you were supposed to know, I would have told you, but it isn't my choice to tell you or not, Sila. I'm not God, and these are God's rules, not mine, and even if you had been told then, or now that you do know, you can't change this or stop it. I know you don't understand any of this right now, but I promise you, someday you will. You can be upset with me now, and believe me, I understand. Look, I know how much you love each other, and know that even after what I have told you, I keep pushing you to take this trip. I hope you will just do it, because it is very important to Jerry, and though I know it doesn't seem terribly important at this moment, I promise it will become one of the most important decisions you will ever make."

She was very quiet, and said in the softest voice, "I don't understand any of this, Karen, but I will definitely let you know."

As the weeks went by, I couldn't stop thinking about Sila's call. I couldn't shake the sadness over her impending loss, and when July first arrived, I found myself saying a silent prayer, hoping they were holding hands on a plane, headed for a month in Italy.

The month was crammed with readings and a quick trip to Los Angeles. Sila and Jerry became the background music in my mind, always followed by a silent prayer. Before I realized it, August had arrived and about ten days into the month, Sila called to give me an update.

She told me she couldn't get my words out of her mind, and they *had* spent the entire month of July in Italy. They had returned about a week earlier and she thanked me for insisting they go, as it turned out to be everything, and more, that Jerry had ever dreamt it would be. They had the most wonderful, memorable time of their lives, and without me even asking, she assured me they had taken at least a thousand pictures.

I felt a profound mixture of sadness and joy as Sila recounted, in great detail, their once-in-a-lifetime trip. For very different reasons, I knew it would be a truly life-changing experience, for both of them. Though they had always shared a deep and abiding love, they had grown even closer during their shared adventure. They got to know each other, and fall in love, all over again.

As she wound down telling me how perfect their trip was, she thanked me for pushing her to fulfill Jerry's dream, and finally that she hoped I was wrong about *the other thing*.

I told her that I hoped I was wrong, too, asking her to please stay in touch with me. She assured me she would. I knew there was nothing I could do to help Sila, nor could I extend the clock, ticking on her remaining days with her beloved husband.

I walked into the kitchen to pour myself a cup of coffee. Taking a seat by the window, I stared out at life in New York, teeming on the streets below.

Though I am but a small part of most people's lives, when the sudden loss of a loved one shows up in a person's reading, the issue is painful, and is the most difficult news for everyone touched by the experience, including me.

With Sila it was no exception. I could see how deeply she and her husband loved each other, how hard they had worked to build the lovely life they shared, and how all of it had been to get to what they perceived as an easier place in life.

Jerry's retirement was supposed to afford them the time to finally enjoy all they had sacrificed for over thirty years. Their unspoken goals were so clear to me: to recapture years of missed laughter and shared pleasures, and to finally slow the pace of their lives. They had been trying to make plans and dream new dreams for this long-awaited chapter in their lives.

In Sila's reading, though I knew their anticipated joy would be short lived, I couldn't tell her. It is never my choice, and when the sudden loss of her beloved husband appeared, it was made clear when the information was coming to me that I was not to tell her.

It was part of her life's journey, and I am never allowed to interfere with God's plans.

Because I deeply understand the impact of loss on our lives, I would never choose to withhold that information, if I had the choice.

The reasons for not telling each person vary, but the easiest explanation is that by them knowing, it will interfere with the lessons God has planned for their life.

I know it is difficult to understand, when you go to a psychic and expect us to just pour everything out in an orderly fashion, but life, and the lessons we all experience, are seldom delivered in a straight line.

I have read for people all over the world and have found that every person's life is different and every emotional experience in their life is interpreted through the filter of their past.

One of the shared lessons of all human beings is learning to integrate each and every emotional experience— love, loss, expectation, joy, disappointment, and the most constant experience, *change*—into our everyday lives.

These are lessons common to us all, though we experience each one of them in a profoundly personal way. The emotional pieces of our lives, and the lessons we learn from them, are what lead us to, and through, the plans God has laid out for our lives.

There have been readings throughout the years when it has been made clear to me that a client's loss was to be part of their reading. This usually occurs when there is unfinished emotional business between my client and the person who is leaving.

Though I have been the messenger of loss on many occasions, it is never easy either way. The purpose of telling someone of an upcoming loss is to offer them the opportunity to heal their heart, and to consciously resolve whatever issues they have been holding on to regarding the person who is leaving.

Sila and Jerry had always taken care of everyone in their families, immediate and extended, yet had given very little to themselves, of time or money. These were not frivolous people; they were planners. In their lives, their dreams would always come true later, and there would always be time for them tomorrow.

Without having spiritual permission to tell Sila that Jerry was leaving, I tried to get her to willingly and lovingly make the commitment for the trip. I tried to encourage her to do something generous and important for her husband, for her marriage, and for her memories.

The astrologer's actions unfortunately took away Sila's freedom of experiencing this lesson without foreknowledge. I was forced to explain my urgency and persistence in her reading, taking away her opportunity to experience this life lesson according to God's plan.

The lesson for Sila was clear: there was no more time. Later was here. If she didn't actively make the plans to turn Jerry's thirty-year-old dream into reality, she would live with guilt and regret for the rest of her life.

I thought about Sila many times over the next few weeks, and by the eighth of September I thought of her more often throughout the days. I began dreading the call that I knew was destined to come on the tenth. That day came and went, however, as did many more days in September, without my receiving the expected call. By the third week in September, I allowed myself to feel that maybe I had been wrong; when it came to this particular reading, all I could think was, "Wouldn't that be wonderful." I prayed that I was wrong on this one.

Each passing day without a phone call made it okay for my spirits to pick up a little, allowing the sense of sadness that had filled my heart to lift. Being wrong in this case would have brought me great joy.

I returned to California on September twenty-fifth, planning a couple of weeks to spend time with my family and friends and to see my clients in Los Angeles.

As the last days of September ticked by, I still hadn't heard from Sila. I had my fingers crossed and took this as a good sign, but I should know better than to ever second-guess what I know in my soul to be true.

The call came on my third day in Los Angeles, late in the afternoon. I heard Sila's clear, strong voice on the other end of the line, and I knew when she said, "Karen?" what this call entailed, before she uttered another word.

I had lived with the expectation of this call for several months, so any preliminary conversation at this point seemed pretty ridiculous. It took everything for me not to burst into tears. I had foolishly allowed myself to hope that this call would never come. "Oh, Sila, I am so sorry. How are you?"

The steadiness of her voice told me she had anticipated this conversation for a long time, too. "You know, Karen, I want to thank you again for pushing me. For making me realize how precious the time I had with Jerry was."

She took a deep breath, hesitating before going on. "I can still hear your words. Do you remember when you told me he wouldn't be here on the ninth of September to go on our trip? Well, about 7:30 on the morning of September ninth, Jerry came down to the kitchen to get some orange juice and coffee. All I heard was a loud 'thud.' I called 911 before I even went in to see what happened, because in my heart I already knew."

Her tears were falling softly now, making her push to get the words out. "He had been fine. You know, he was in perfect health, Karen, but the doctor said he was gone before he hit the floor. I am so thankful he didn't have any pain, and of course for our trip. He couldn't talk about anything else since we got back."

Now I was crying, too. "I am so sorry, honey. How are you doing? I was so praying I was wrong, and when I didn't hear from you on the tenth, I thought maybe I was wrong, and Jerry was fine."

The strength had returned to her voice. "I thought about you every day, but I couldn't call you right away. I needed a little time to work through everything, but I'm doing much better now. I have good days and bad days, and I don't know why, but there is a part of me that wishes I hadn't known Jerry was going to die. I want you to know that now, after everything, in my heart I understand why you weren't supposed to tell me, and I'm sorry for making you do it. I just wanted to thank you for being honest with me, even though I wish I hadn't known."

I still think about Sila. Her reading and her experience taught me so much about the true value of time spent with the people you love, and how truly priceless a few small moments can be.

I received the gift of understanding priorities, understanding that nothing in life can replace love, or time, and that we have the potential to learn our greatest lessons during our deepest moments of despair.

When I think about Sila, my heart is a peaceful place now. I think of all that she and her husband shared, and how truly blessed they were to have each other for over thirty years. I know that Jerry visits Sila often, and that now she knows for certain that he never really left.

The Bookie

For many years I had friends, a married couple, who owned a dental supply company. It was 1975, and my friends' company carried the dental porcelain I coated my very long nails with so they wouldn't break.

Their office was located in a San Fernando Valley industrial park: a nondescript series of five small corrugated-metal warehouses, strung together by a common walkway and delivery ramp. They were nothing fancy but highly functional, all housing wholesale businesses of one sort or another.

My friends mentioned that a friend of theirs wanted a reading. They told me he was a nice man who owned an electrical supply company in the same industrial complex.

A few weeks later I was running out of dental porcelain, so I called and said I was coming by to pick some up. When I arrived, we sat in their office chatting over coffee.

They reminded me about their neighbor's ongoing request for a reading, asking if I had time since I was already there.

Before I could answer, the husband grabbed the phone and said, "Let me see if he's next door right now." He was, and he instructed them to bring me over.

We finished our coffee, exited the delivery door at the rear of the building, and turned right. We walked two spaces down and entered their friend's business.

Nothing seemed unusual; however, I immediately felt a very peculiar energy in the place. There were ten or twelve tall metal shelving units, about six feet long, all on an angle to the right. For an electrical supply company, it was so immaculate you could eat off the floors. There were boxes, all of identical size and proportion, lined up on every shelf.

It struck me that for an electrical parts business, this place was exceptionally clean, unusually quiet, and as orderly as a library. There were no customers digging through the oddly identical boxes, nor did there appear to be any employees.

We walked past all the shelving to a small, rectangular, glass-enclosed office. It was located in the left rear of the building with a bird's-eye view of the entire place.

A short, chubby man with thinning gray hair, in a polo shirt and cardigan sweater, sporting Sansabelt slacks, emerged from the office. He looked like he had just stepped off a golf course. Well into his sixties and standing no more than 5'6" with a Humpty Dumpty–type body, there was a kind, rather grandfatherly air to him.

My friends left me in what they thought was his good care. Waving goodbye, and with a very gallant sweep, he opened the office door, directing me to a seat with the slightest nod. Standing still, he made sure I was seated before moving from the door. With a slight smile on his face, he entered the small space, closing and purposely locking the door behind him.

With obvious comfort he slid into his big leather chair. He raised his gaze, intently watching my face as I looked at the doorknob and the lock.

Waving my hand back toward the glass behind my head and looking directly at him, I nervously asked, "Bulletproof?"

With the slightest nod and a smile that had become more of a smirk, he said, "You're a smart girl. Yep, all of this is bulletproof, every bit of it."

All of a sudden I was terribly thirsty and a bit unnerved. As I was about to find out, *nothing* with this grandfatherly looking gentleman was as it appeared to be.

He didn't utter a word, nor did the smile ever leave his lips. As he settled his ample body into the chair, his eyes never left my face.

I took a deep breath, wondering what in the world I had just stepped into.

He could see that I was visibly uncomfortable. Un-comfortable with him, uncomfortable with being locked in his bulletproof office, and very uncomfortable that I didn't understand what he wanted from me.

After a couple of moments, he attempted to make small talk by offering me coffee. I barely had the "Yes, black, thank you" out of my mouth when he twirled around in his chair to a rather compact coffeemaker set-up, located directly behind his chair.

He clearly didn't want me to leave.

He kept staring and smiling at me as I sipped my coffee. Reluctantly, I asked if he still wanted to go ahead with the reading.

Without hesitation he said, "Absolutely, I have waited a very long time to meet you." His words were warm, almost friendly, but his eyes were like a shark's: dark, cold, and emotionless.

I closed my eyes for a moment to clear my mind, opening them to find that he hadn't even blinked. I cleared my throat and started his reading. I talked in depth about his close-knit family, his beloved grandchildren, his mother's health issues, and a problem he had with the circulation in his left leg, methodically delving into every area of his *personal* life.

In all the years I have been doing this work, I have never been shy about telling a client anything I see. Nor do I normally, unless it is clear to me when I begin a person's reading, ever withhold information, no matter how difficult a topic it is, but this reading felt different. Though he appeared harmless, this man felt dangerous to me. There were areas of this man's life that I didn't want to look at. I didn't want to know this man, or his business. As I do in every reading, when I was done and had said everything I had to say, I asked him if there was anything else he wanted to know about.

I barely had the question out of my mouth as his words tumbled on top of mine.

He had just been waiting for the opportunity. "Yes, I want you to talk to me about my business."

With him knowing that I had purposely avoided the subject, there was nothing else for me to say except, "Well, since we both know you aren't *really* in the electrical-parts supply business, exactly which business would you like to talk about?"

Still fixed on me, and looking for some interest on my part, he casually said, "I would like for you to talk about *sports*."

Well, that was an easy one for me. Since I knew absolutely nothing about sports, I relaxed a little bit. Comfortably, I said, "Sports? Oh, I'm sorry. I don't know anything about sports."

That wasn't about to deter him a bit, so we were going to have a short game of playing cat and mouse. He leaned forward, reassessing me, his voice taking on a more menacing tone. "Sure you do. You know, *sports*. Like *sports* betting, *sports* gambling. You know … *sports*, Karen."

So that was it, sports betting! I just had to decipher exactly what he thought I knew about sports or betting. Neither of these were things that had ever even crossed my mind, as they were subjects far removed from my life.

I was looking at him as it slowly dawned on me. Oh, my God! He was *a bookie*! I mean, a big-time bookie! *This* was his *real* business. He wasn't just some guy who managed the neighborhood bowling-league money. In his world he was a serious businessman, and there was a lot of money on the line.

He proceeded to explain in great detail the exact nature of his business: what it really was, and to clear up any question I might have had regarding *exactly* what he wanted from me. He stressed his importance to me that *he* was the guy who handled *all* of the sports bets.

Almost every dollar that was placed or paid out on sports in Southern California went through his hands. He wanted an edge. Like I said, in his mind, this was big business, and he was right: it was very big.

I fidgeted in my chair and nervously said, "Umm, I'm sorry, but I don't do sports."

My obvious discomfort didn't move him in the least. He clearly didn't care how I felt. This man was used to getting what he wanted, and my ethics were of no concern to him.

He brushed my refusal off as though I hadn't said it. Narrowing his stare, and with the slight hint of a threat in his voice, he continued, "But you *will* do it for me." It wasn't a question. For him, it was a statement of fact. All pretense of warmth had vanished pretty quickly as he continued talking about his business. The more he talked, the colder and more aggressive he became. He didn't raise his voice, but his tone had changed. It had become steely, threatening, and dark.

There was a fearful chill circling around me. I am sure, like all sharks, he could smell my fear, and there was nothing I could do to prevent it. No sense of false bravado was going to stop this man. He had a plan, and that was the way it was.

I stiffened in my chair as he continued, "You know I take the bets, and there's a bunch of games this weekend, so why don't we do this."

My complete lack of interest didn't mean a thing to him as he kept laying out his plan. "I'll give you the list, and you'll pick the games for me."

It was so simple for him. He delivered this information to me as if I actually had a voice in his plan.

Again his tone changed. Now leaning in closer and looking at the floor, he continued speaking to me in this conspiratorial "we're in this together" or "now that you're on board," buddy-buddy kind of manner. The only thing he lacked was sincerity. He made my flesh crawl.

He leaned back in his chair, pulling out the top desk drawer, sliding a neatly typed sheet of paper out onto the space in front of him. Upside down, it looked to me like what we now call a spreadsheet. He picked it up, running his eyes over the columns as though trying to make a decision. In one swift move, he turned it right side up, pushing it in front of me.

I picked up the paper and he reached over, snatching it out of my hand to place it back on the desk in front of me. "Leave it there!" he barked. "You don't have to hold it, just look at it."

I stared at the paper without a word. I felt like a statue sitting there, motionless and cold. I still had no idea what he wanted, or what this piece of paper had to do with me.

More quietly, while tapping on the paper, he informed me, "There are ten or twelve games this weekend. You'll do those."

I tried pleading ignorance. "But I don't even know what teams are playing. What do you want from me?"

He was not convinced and was getting angry. He started poking his index finger repeatedly on the paper. "I want you to pick the winners, so just look at the paper, do whatever it is you do, and put checks next to the winners, okay? It's pretty simple."

Frozen in place, I lowered my eyes, focusing on this piece of paper with names and boxes all over it.

Exasperated by my lack of enthusiasm and ongoing denial of any sports knowledge, he watched me like a hawk. Reaching into his pocket, he pulled out a Montblanc pen, holding it up in front of me over the mystery paper on the desk. I didn't take it. His eyes narrowed as he started jabbing the air with the pen. Just as suddenly he stopped, holding the pen very still between his thumb and forefinger, in front of my face. In a low voice, through clenched teeth, he said, "Take it."

I reluctantly took the pen, still looking down at the paper, and said clearly, "Just this once."

I started checking off the teams that would win; this took about three minutes. I recapped the pen, looked over the paper one last time, and slid it and the pen back across the desk.

Snatching both of them up in one move, he leaned back in his chair. Unconsciously poking at his lip with the pen, he held the paper in front of his face, seeming to memorize every checkmark.

I stood up, ready to leave. As far as I was concerned, we were finished, and I would never have to deal with this scary little man ever again. No goodbye seemed necessary, but I needed to make sure he understood my intention, "Remember, I said it was just this once."

Seemingly unfazed by my words, he stood up, silently slipping the precious paper into the top drawer. The grandfather in him magically reappeared as he reached into his pocket to pay me for the reading. Peeling off the bills and counting them into my hand, he got a strange look in his eyes that made me very uncomfortable. Softly pressing the money into my palm, he smiled. "We'll see about that now, won't we?"

I didn't say a word.

As I am sure he had done a thousand times, he unlocked and opened his bulletproof office door, putting on his gentleman's mask to escort me out.

With my heart racing, I practically ran out of the office. Looking straight ahead and placing careful distance between us, I crossed the warehouse aiming for the door. I wanted to pretend that I had never met him, to be away from his energy and just feel safe again. I stiffly turned left out the door I had entered over an hour earlier. Naively, I had stepped into this little man's very dark world, and wanted no part of it, or him. Breathing a little heavier, my pace picked up as I reentered my friends' business.

Waving and smiling, the wife gushed, "So how was it? Isn't he the *nicest* man? He's always so sweet. We just love him!" She never noticed my distress.

I realized at that moment that my lovely friends didn't know. They had no idea who this man really was. They had been innocently charmed by his wife's homemade pastries and pasta sauce, and had been smitten by his well-crafted grandfatherly persona.

As casually as I could muster, I inquired, "So how long have you known him?"

Her husband emerged from the back of the ware-house; they looked at each other as he counted in his head. "Hmm, it has to be over four years now. Isn't he just the nicest guy, Karen?"

Trying to find an appropriate response, I chose to ignore all their delusions about him, and ethically was not comfortable with revealing his true nature. I would never be able to tell them who he really was, so I kept it simple. "Thanks so much for the referral. I deeply appreciate it." It was apparent to me that they saw him through very different eyes, and as I knew that they were in no danger, it wasn't my job to clear up their misconception about him.

When you read my next statement, please remember that I have changed the names of every client in every story in this book. Though I am sharing their true stories, I will never reveal any of my clients' real names or true identities.

I have never been the town crier. I made it a policy when I started giving readings never to reveal a client's personal life, their business issues, or their reading to another. Regardless of how a client comes to me, what is discussed in a reading is between us. I deeply respect people's privacy, and if a client wants to tell someone that they have seen me, and what their reading entails, it is their right to do that. It isn't mine.

I tucked my issues with their neighbor away in my head, grateful to be done with him. We chatted for a few more minutes. I paid for my dental porcelain and hurried to my car. I couldn't wait to get home and take a shower. It was the perfect way to completely cleanse his energy from around me. After a long, hot shower, I would be done with him.

The weekend was filled with several readings and a casual dinner party with some friends. The Bookie never crossed my mind. I was a happy girl. I was in my early twenties at the time, and my mother lived with me in a lovely house in Studio City. It had a big yellow country kitchen, a huge backyard with a built-in brick barbecue, plenty of room for my dog and my friends, and space to accommodate the meditation classes I taught on a regular basis.

I was very happily supporting my mother, but carrying the house and all the bills connected with it had become quite a financial juggling act. I was happy, but getting very stressed out over money issues. I was overjoyed to have my mother living with me. She was a lovely, funny, smart woman, and my best friend. We just adored each other's company. She had worked her entire life, and only stopped working when her health dictated otherwise.

She had never been a high-maintenance woman, emotionally or financially. She wasn't spoiled and had never put herself first. She had never had it easy, and there was so much I wanted to do for her, so I always put her first. I loved making sure she was comfortable and never wanted her to worry about money issues, no matter what pressure I was under. She had never complained about doing without for herself when I was growing up, so I never complained to her now. My wish from childhood had been to spoil her, to give her the support and freedom she had always given me.

This was a particularly rough period for me financially. I earned money in one hand, with it quickly going out the other. I worked every day and never turned down a reading or the opportunity to help someone who needed me. Having friends over for a barbecue or dinner was always relaxing for me, and since all my friends loved my mother too, it was a simple pleasure that we both enjoyed. This was one of those relaxing weekends. Little did I know at the time, but it would be the last evening I would truly relax for quite a while.

The Bookie was the furthest thing from my thoughts as Monday morning unfolded. I set up a couple of doctor's appointments for my mother, did a phone reading for a client from Houston, and sat down to juggle the never-ending pile of bills. It was a typical Monday morning for me.

The phone rang, and it was my friend from the dental supply company. The husband sounded ecstatic. "Boy, Karen, you sure made some impression on our friend!

He was waiting at the door this morning for your phone number, so I gave him your card. We knew you wouldn't mind, because he's such a nice man." I thanked him and kept it short.

I hung up the phone, hoping the Bookie wouldn't call, even though I knew he certainly would. A few hours later, my mother answered the phone, and it was him.

He knew that I didn't want to talk to him, so he leapt right in. "Karen, please don't hang up! Just hear me out. I have a proposition for you."

I was furious inside, but kept it civil. "I'm not interested in any proposition from you."

He wasn't giving up. "Please, just pick the games for me."

My voice was flat. "I told you. I don't do sports."

He laughed, "Well, for a girl who doesn't do sports, you picked more winners than I've picked in twenty-seven years in this business. I'll make it well worth your time."

I couldn't ignore the stack of bills in front of me, and I knew the twelve dollars in my bank account wasn't going to cover them. I was silent for a long time. A loud argument raged in my head. This was simply *not* a solution for me.

He was very smart man. He didn't say a word, and waited for me to speak.

As I stared at my bills, the pressure and the reality of my financial situation finally spoke for me. "What's your proposition?"

It flowed right off his tongue. "I'll pay you fifty dollars per game, and all you have to do is pick the games for me. Win or lose, you get paid."

I was silent, but I could hear him holding his breath. If I didn't know better, I would have thought he had his fingers crossed, making silent wishes while he made his pitch to me.

In 1975, fifty dollars per game was a lot of money. If I did it for just one season, I could pay off all my bills and make our lives easier.

I was dry and unemotional. "Okay. Here's how this will work. I don't want to see *you*. Ever. You will have someone drop off cash in my mailbox every morning. You get one phone call a day, and at the end of the season, you can never call me again. Do you understand? By the way, this is *non-negotiable*."

He was thrilled. "You got it, Karen! Any way you want it, but can we talk again at the end of the season before you just say no?"

"No, we can't!" He heard me, and stopped pushing.

I didn't like this man. I didn't respect him, and I definitely didn't trust him.

He did keep his end of the bargain, though. Every morning during football season, the Bookie had some big bruiser of a guy drop off an envelope in my mailbox. He never missed a day and always made sure that the guy had delivered the money before he called.

One morning I decided to peek out my front window, just to see who was coming to my house every morning. The guy looked like a boxer, big and mean. After seeing him, I walked straight into my big yellow kitchen and sat there for a long time, drinking a cup of coffee and holding my mother's hand.

I never peeked out at him again. I didn't want him to know anything about me because I wanted to protect my mother and myself, and the only way I could do that was to make sure he never knew what either of us looked like.

I set a schedule with the Bookie, one that I thought I could live with. My real problem in working with him in any way was that my work had never been about money for me. My work is, and always has been, my soul's calling.

I had never, ever done a reading with money as my motivation, and I was having a terrible emotional time living with my decision. Unfortunately, I knew at this point that I had no choice. Every day I thought of backing out, but every time I did, the face of the delivery guy popped up in front of me. If that wasn't enough to make me honor my agreement, I could vividly recall the feeling of terror I experienced sitting locked in a bulletproof office, with a shark behind the desk.

The Bookie was on his best behavior with me. He would call me every morning, read off the names of the teams, and I would pick the winners. It was a simple formula that worked for him. He was very happy with the arrangement. I could barely live with myself.

Every morning at the designated time, the phone would ring and, even before I heard his voice, every muscle in my body tightened up. It stayed that way until the end of football season. As promised, I picked the games for one football season. The Bookie made a lot of money, and in turn he made my life a little easier financially.

I have to hand it to him: at the end of the season he made me a second offer, an attempt to get me to keep picking games for him. He offered me double the money.

My answer was still, and would always be from that moment on … *no*. Surprisingly, he was very gracious and said he understood. What he didn't, and couldn't, understand was that for me, there was *no amount of money* he, or anyone else, could pay me to do it ever again. I could never, nor would I ever, do it or anything like it again.

The price I paid emotionally, just to pay my bills, can never be measured. I am clear every single day of my life that for a few weeks out of my life, I made the decision to compromise myself, and my ethics, for money.

Some people can look at it as just a business deal, and I know that the Bookie certainly did. He was paying for my services, but for me it was a profoundly different experience. It took me going through some very difficult financial situations over the years to truly realize that I would never again do anything *just* for money.

I love my work and my relationship with God, and there is no question in my soul why I do this work. The truth is, we all *know* when we are doing something alien to our nature, and *this* was completely alien to mine.

My feelings are never ambiguous and are always very clear, yet just this once I consciously chose to ignore them, and I couldn't stand the way this decision made me feel, even for a few short weeks. It was for all the wrong reasons, and against everything I have ever believed in.

All these years later, I can look at the story through different eyes. I know why I made the agreement with this man. I can rationalize my decision with the knowledge that I had to pay my bills, but even knowing that will never really make it okay for me.

This experience taught me so much about life and the choices we make. It made me realize that any issue or problem that can only be solved with money is not really a problem.

It is true, the Bookie made a lot of money taking my advice, but the lesson I learned from him was priceless.

8

Blood on the Wall

Throughout the years I have been giving readings, it has always been my preference for clients to record their readings. I think of this as a reference tool so my clients can go back and clarify the difference between what I actually said and what they thought I said. I have learned many things about people through my work and the distinct difference between what I say in someone's reading and what the client wants to hear. I have learned that many of us are simply attached to the belief of how we want our lives to be, and when I see unanticipated changes in a reading for someone, especially life-changing ones, sometimes the client will just dig their heels in and choose not to hear what I have said.

In the mid-1970s, I had a client who was a very prominent set designer. Anita had exquisite taste, and was responsible for creating the look and feel of many of the high-budget, star-studded films in Hollywood. She and her equally lovely but non-Hollywood-industry husband lived in a townhouse complex in Studio City.

Part of the great love and respect I have for my work is that each person's life truly is unique and beautiful in its own way. Every single reading is different, and no two people *or* two lives are exactly alike; *that* is a fact.

This gracious Southern lady's readings over the years were different for me in another way. They were unusual, in that her readings always followed a particular pattern and felt as though they were being directed from another place. I would start every reading with the issues concerning her private life and weave my way through, describing in great detail the people I saw her dealing with and the films I saw her being offered over the next several months.

I have had the pleasure of seeing many of the films I had described in her readings over the years. It is an almost otherworldly experience to see what lived only in my head, brought to life on the screen by her amazing talent.

At the time of this particular reading, Anita had been my client for many years. She was not only my client, but we liked each other as human beings.

When I looked at her in a reading, I could see her sweet and loving nature, along with the warmth and love she carried in her heart. I never thought of her as the overworked, deadline-pressured businesswoman she became on a movie set, even though that showed up in her readings, too.

In this particular reading, I started with some surprising news. "Wow! You guys are moving. I see you selling your townhouse and buying another house in February. It's not in the same area, and it isn't a townhouse. It looks like a big Spanish stucco house in the hills."

She had no interest in hearing this. "We aren't interested in selling the townhouse right now, Karen. So that's not possible."

I could see the house clearly and was very certain they were moving. I continued with my detailed description. "Well, I hear what you are saying, but I still see you moving. What a beautiful house: well built, full of character, *and* you'll get a great deal on it. I keep seeing the number: $278,000. It's an older, thick-walled, Spanish stucco home, built in the 1920s." The details were pouring out of me. "I keep seeing dark-red Mexican paver tiles on the floors and a spiral staircase as you enter that will take you downstairs to the personal living areas. I see very ornate doorknobs and fittings throughout the house like the old-fashioned ones, but they all look like they've been painted over. It has beautiful ceilings with carved relief work and hand-done woodwork throughout the house, but unfortunately it looks like they have repeatedly painted over everything. The house needs a lot of work, but you are so good at all that stuff. You'll love it."

No matter what I saw about the house, Anita didn't have any intention of moving; and, thinking that I must not have heard her the first time, she became insistent.

"We aren't moving, Karen. You know we are very happy where we are, so I don't know where this house stuff is coming from, but believe me, you are way off-base on this one."

I was still busy walking around the house in my head, and despite her protests I continued describing each room in detail. "I know, Anita, and I know you don't plan to move, but you have had enough readings with me to know that I see what I see, and I see you guys moving into this house! It is as clear as a bell. It's built on a hill, with big windows running the entire length of the kitchen at the back of the house."

I couldn't stop, because the house and its surroundings were crystal clear. "What a beautiful view! I see you standing at the kitchen sink, looking out at this endless view of the mountains. I do have to tell you, though: there is an earthquake fault running directly under the kitchen that they have tried very hard to bury. It will take four title searches to find it, but the title company *will* find it."

She was quiet now, allowing me to keep talking. "This is really weird: it shows up as a cloud on the title, which will be a little confusing, but *keep* looking. I promise, you *will* find it. It feels like it will cost $70,000 to shore it up, and I know that sounds like a lot, but even with the additional $70,000, this house is a great investment."

Anita knew from our history together to just let me finish. If she didn't, I would be like a dog with a bone until I had given her all the information she needed. I would just keep going back to it in the reading.

I could see that all of the details regarding this house had no relevance in her life at that moment, but I also knew what I saw, and that she would need this information much sooner than she ever imagined.

My job as a psychic is not to pick and choose what to tell a person. The information in a reading is to help them, and is not mine to keep. I respect that sometimes clients don't want to hear what I see for them. Often, information is provided for an upcoming situation, and it is always important, but it will have no meaning in their life at that moment. I am quite sensitive to the discomfort an unanticipated issue can cause in a person's life, but I must clearly convey what I see, whether the client wants to hear it at the time or not. I find that inevitably it winds up being the critical information, with the exact details necessary, to identify and define the situation I have foreseen. The client just doesn't know it at the time.

Though it came as no surprise to me, within a few months Anita and her husband were being pushed to move from two sides. Their financial planner and their accountant told them that their tax bracket had changed, and they needed to sell their townhouse and step up. Reluctantly, they contacted their broker, making the wise decision to start their search for a new home. Within a few days the broker had located a house in the Hollywood Hills for them to look at.

Anita's voice was very excited on the phone. "You were right, Karen. As much as I hate to say it, we're moving! I should know better after all this time; maybe one of these days I'll learn just to listen to you. My accountant said we have to move quickly, and we've already looked at a house in the hills that we're thinking of writing an offer on. I'm going back there today because I want to be sure, and would like you to go with me? Can you come?"

I couldn't wait to see the beautiful house that I had described in her reading. "Of course I'll go. I'm sure I'll recognize the house the minute I see it. Want to pick me up?"

Relieved that I agreed to go on such short notice, Anita said, "I'm sure you will. That's why I want you to come with me. I'll pick you up in an hour. I just have to pick up the keys."

On time as always, she wasted no time taking off in the direction of the Hollywood Hills. We chatted animatedly about the house as she drove, turning here and there, climbing up and around, into the winding hills above the city.

Approaching a curve on Tareco Drive, I saw the house and began pointing at it with great excitement. "There's your house! I knew I'd recognize it."

In an instant, her body tensed and her entire demeanor darkened as she continued rounding the curve. "That's not the house, Karen. I don't know anything about that house. Our house is up the street, right over here."

Now I was totally confused. "No, honey, *that* is the house I see you buying," I said, with my finger still pointing back over my shoulder. Why would she drive past the house I saw in my head? Slowly I lowered my hand, not understanding why she wanted me there.

Our uncomfortable silence continued for another long block until, tensely clutching the steering wheel, Anita carefully pulled up in front of a house. It was an exact copy of the house I saw her buying. Only this one was much smaller.

Like sudden strangers, we quickly exited the car. Anita hurried up the walk, leaving me standing outside the car, looking back up the street behind us. I was certain these two homes had been designed and built by the same person, except this one was half the size and definitely not her house.

I followed her lead to the door, the discomfort between us continuing as she nervously fumbled with the key. Stiff-backed and emotionally frazzled, she finally managed to get the front door open.

I trailed her into the house, noticing all the details I had accurately described in her reading: the huge Mexican paver tiles in the foyer and a beautiful spiral staircase to the right, leading downstairs to the personal areas of the house. I took it all in, but it still didn't feel right. I knew something was terribly wrong with this beautiful house. I just had to figure out what it was.

In silence we passed the stairs, making a right into the living room, a huge fireplace taking up most of the wall facing us. Anita quickly glanced at me, hoping for some reaction, but the only thing I felt was the continuing discomfort that had started a block away.

Trying to make conversation and elicit a weather report from me on the house, Anita headed toward the kitchen talking a mile a minute, but without conviction. "Amazing, isn't it? I couldn't believe it when we first walked in. It has all the things you said it would have. Did you notice the Mexican pavers in the entry hall?"

I had definitely noticed, but obviously with a lot less enthusiasm than she was looking for. I was also completely aware of how crazy I was about to sound to her. "Yeah, I sure did notice them, and it *is* a beautiful house." I paused, searching for the right words. "But Anita, this *isn't* the house that I see you living in. Something is very wrong here."

The forced smile left her face, and almost imperceptibly she slumped. A forced defiance was in her voice. "What do you mean, *wrong*? This *is* the house."

Now in the kitchen, she walked over to one of the doors, looking at me while groping for the doorknob. "How can you say that something is wrong? Even the doorknobs and fittings are the old-fashioned kind!" Her eyes pleaded with me to change my mind. "Look!"

I was getting more and more uncomfortable, with frustration layering my words. "I know, I see them, but these are all like new. The ones that I saw in your reading were painted over. *You* would have to strip them down, and *then* they would look like that one! Not when you moved in, remember? They've redone everything here. None of this is done in the house I saw."

Dredging up a glimmer of resistance and hoping I would come around, Anita continued, "Will you at least *look* at the rest of the house?" The pleading returned to her eyes. "The master bedroom is just gorgeous. Before you say this isn't our house, please will you at least look at it?"

I didn't like what I was feeling, and I liked it even less because I couldn't put my finger on where this feeling was coming from.

We slowly wandered through the rest of the top floor. Anita kept talking, nervously pointing out all the details I had enumerated in her reading.

Slowly, I walked behind her, with a sense of dread building in me with every room we entered. I didn't have a lot to say to her about this house, except that the energy was stifling for me, and before I could explain it to her, I needed to know where it came from. What had happened here, and which room had poisoned the energy in this beautiful house? When I entered it, I would know.

We finally meandered back to the foyer. Looking down at the large, dark red tiles under our feet, we slowly descended the wide spiral staircase, the last step leaving us off at the opening of a long hallway. We stopped at the foot of the staircase, taking it all in. For a moment there was peace between us, looking straight ahead to the surprise at the end of the hall. There, with the sun shining through, was a set of perfectly romantic French doors. From where we stood, we could see that they opened up to the magic of sunlight, dancing off the surface of a shimmering blue pool and a never-ending view. Neither of us moved, touched by the unexpected beauty of this extraordinary sight.

Talking to me over her shoulder as we started moving down the hall, Anita said, "This *is* the house, Karen.

I mean, it has to be; it has every detail. How could it not be our house?"

I chose my words with great care. "Yes, Anita, you're right, it certainly does appear to have everything, but I still don't see you in this house."

Anita knew what those words meant, coming from me. If I didn't *see* her in this house, she knew something was going to happen to prevent it. She was wound so tight over the move already that I could feel her fear going into overdrive, imagining all sorts of things.

I felt terrible telling her this, but I had no choice, and I couldn't define the reasons for her until they were clear in my mind. I knew in my heart that whatever it was, it was a truth she wouldn't want to hear.

The door to the master bedroom was at the end of the hall on the left. The room wrapped around to include a sitting area with the beautiful French doors, but until I was standing at the bedroom entrance, I didn't realize that the endless view was an optical illusion. It was actually in the shape of a very large, long L, creating a pretty amazing view from the foot of the stairs.

Anita stepped through the doorway, practically floating into the center of an extra big, beautiful bedroom. The walls had been painted just a hint of peach, with a stark white ceiling.

I was barely inside the door when I stopped abruptly, suddenly unable to take another step. Frozen in place, I couldn't stop staring at the center of the large wall facing the bedroom door.

Anita was twirling around in the center of the room. "Isn't this room just gorgeous, Karen?"

I couldn't share her appreciation of the beauty, and was, for possibly the first time in my life, at a complete loss for words.

Anita stopped twirling, noticing the look on my face, following the line of my stare to the wall, trying desperately to see what I was so fixated on. Clearly hypnotized by the beauty of this house, she glared at me, no longer able to mask her frustration. Planting herself in the middle of the room, she placed her hands on her hips and asked, "*What* are you staring at?"

Pointing at the center of the wall, my words came out stilted and flat. "There's blood on that wall."

Her eyes became enormous as she whipped around looking at the wall. Her hysteria rose. "Where do you see blood? What are you talking about? Can't you see it's just been painted?"

I was still unable to move, or to take my eyes off the wall. "Yes, I see that, but there is blood all over that wall."

Wild-eyed, Anita rapidly moved toward the target of my stare and began running her hands up and down the wall, with panic creeping into her voice. "There's no blood on this wall, Karen! Can't you see the wall has just been painted? Where do you see blood?"

Now I knew what had happened in this house, and though she didn't want to hear it, I had to tell her. "I know you can't see it, but someone was murdered here, and there is blood all over that wall. You need to find out who was murdered in this room"—I pointed—"against *that* wall. I'm sorry, Anita, but I can't stay in this house. I need to get out of here now."

Heading back up the hall to the staircase, half talking to myself, I said, "Now I know why I can't breathe in here, and I promise you one thing, *you* are *never* moving into this house."

I ran up the stairs as though I was being chased. Gasping for air, I scrambled out the front door, continuing up the walkway, finally arriving at the car. I couldn't even bring myself to look back at the house, and for what seemed like a very long time, I just stood next to the car, trying to calm my racing heart.

Anita emerged from the walkway, looking at me like I had suddenly lost my mind. In the car, her fear finally surfaced. "What in the world happened to you back there? All I wanted you to do was look at the house we are buying, and you've been acting strange from the minute we drove up here. It's kind of freaking me out, Karen. What happened to you?"

I calmly tried to explain it to her. "This isn't your house, Anita, and I know I keep saying this to you, but even before I got to the bedroom, I told you that I didn't *ever* see you living there. I am telling you that someone was definitely murdered in that bedroom! I know you want me to tell you that this is the place, but I'm sorry, I can't. I know what I see, and I have to tell you the truth. I'm sorry, I just can't tell you what you want to hear."

On the drive home, I told her how I felt. She had been completely convinced before we got there that this was the house, and through her eyes it did appear to have every detail that I had described in her reading. So, in her mind, it had to be this house. To her it was absolutely perfect. I was the problem, and because she needed to rationalize my strange reaction, she simply decided that I must be crazy. As we drove down the mountain, my mind was spinning. I was desperately trying to find a way to express my concerns about the house. I chose instead to listen quietly as she repeatedly tried to convince me, and I agreed that all of the things she said were true. However, the harder she pushed, the more certain I became. She was never buying, nor moving into, that house.

The overwhelming energy carried within that house, and the powerful feelings of darkness and murder, were suffocating for me. I was simply amazed that she couldn't feel it, too. I was also confused about the exactness of all the details from her reading and my deepening certainty that this was absolutely not the house I had described. The logical part of my mind knew that it certainly should be the house, if in fact everything I had described was there, so none of it was making sense to me.

I started going over the details, one by one, asking if she was certain that *everything* I had said about the house fit perfectly. "Okay, I know it has the doorknobs and fittings, even though they aren't covered with paint like I saw them, and it also has the Mexican pavers and the fireplace. Do you remember what else I said it would have?"

She appeared more relaxed now, thinking she had talked me into changing my mind. "Well, there are a couple of big things that don't exactly fit what you said. One is the price. Remember you kept saying $278,000? Well, you were way off on that one, by about $40,000, and that thing you kept saying about a fault under the kitchen?" Suddenly she realized the seriousness of what she'd said. "Does there still feel like there's a fault under the kitchen?" She didn't really want me to answer, so she kept talking. "No, of course there isn't, so I'm sure you were off on that one, too, but everything else fits."

The shift in her tone and attitude made me laugh. We had known each other a long time, and she knew that when I saw something with such clarity and with so much detail I was never changing my mind, no matter how hard she pushed or disagreed with me. I would never have said this wasn't her house if I were not absolutely certain.

I addressed every point. "So, let's see, all the little details sort of fit, but none of the big ones? I must admit, in your reading I never saw a murder or blood on the wall in the bedroom, but, Anita, all of it just feels wrong, and to answer your last question: yes, I still feel there is a fault running under the kitchen. Not under the kitchen in *this* house, but absolutely in the house you are buying, so I don't know what else to tell you." There was something else really bothering me: I couldn't get the house on the Tareco Drive curve out of my mind.

Though she didn't show it, I knew that she was still deeply upset and simply didn't know what to do. My insistence about nothing being what it appeared to be with this house was driving her crazy. First she is told she has to move; then she thinks she has found the house I described in her reading. She takes me to the house, and I tell her there has been a murder committed in the master bedroom. Who wouldn't be upset with all of that going on?

I gently tried again. "I know how stressful all of this is, but before you make a final decision, will you hear me out?" She looked like she was about to cry. "Please, I'm begging you to check out the history of this house first. I know you think I'm just being crazy, but have I ever steered you wrong? I know what I feel, sweetheart, and I promise you there was a murder, against the wall, in that bedroom. I know you don't want to hear this, but I know what I feel, and I know what I saw. If I'm wrong, I will apologize up one side and down the other, and will never ask you to do anything ever again. Please?" Anita fought the tears filling her eyes, but I knew she needed to hear all of it. "And if I'm right about the blood, the second thing I want you to do is find out about the house on the curve. Remember the big one I kept pointing at?"

She was really angry with me, but I continued, "Please, don't be angry, and just ask your broker to find out about that house. I know you don't want to, but do it just to amuse me, okay? I know none of this makes any sense to you right now, but I know what I feel, and there is something so wrong about that house. Please, for yourself, check it out."

With barely a goodbye, she dropped me off, refusing to promise me anything. I could only hope that she listened and would at least investigate what I said about blood on the bedroom wall. I prayed she would protect herself, and her husband, from living in the energy where a murder had been committed, and not wind up shooting the messenger in the process.

She was so angry at me that I didn't really expect to hear from her for a while, but a couple of weeks later she called. "Okay, you win! I give up! I did it, and I'm sorry I was so upset with you over the house. I was so freaked out that I didn't ever want to talk to you again, but the truth is I couldn't get the look on your face in the bedroom out of my mind. So in spite of myself, I heard what you told me in the car."

I laughed, "I knew you were really mad at me, and I felt terrible, but you know me, Anita. I can't pretend I feel something I don't. What made you finally check it out?"

Her voice was sweet and playful. "I'm telling you it was the look on your face. That look forced me to do a little research on that beautiful house. Well, I almost fainted when I found out that a gangster had lived in that house, and just like you said, he was murdered in his bed against that very bedroom wall. It's all pretty weird, Karen, but the *really* weird part for me is that he was killed many years ago. Long before either of us were ever born. That wall must have been painted over at least a dozen times since the blood was there. How in the world did you see it?"

I was so relieved. "I don't know, but it was as clear as a bell to me. Now you know why I was so weird in there. I'm just happy you found out and have stopped trying to make it fit the reading, and I'm really happy you aren't buying it. You aren't, are you?"

Anita laughed, "Oh, not a chance, we're kind of still looking, but the other thing you said that bugged me was about that other house, you know, the one on the curve? Well, I finally broke down and have my broker checking into it, but I don't think it's on the market."

I was a happy girl. "It feels empty to me, like it's been waiting for you. Will you let me know what happens?" I knew that the house on the curve was the house from her reading.

The next call from Anita was great news. "Okay, Miss Karen, you're batting a thousand this time. The house on the curve has been empty for years, but it isn't on the market. It's in some kind of a trust, and wait, before you say anything, I'm pushing my broker to see if they want to sell. I have my fingers crossed."

I reassured her that they would be willing to sell, and I gave her one final reminder. "Just remember: $278,000. That's the number. You should be hearing from your broker in the next couple of days. Please let me know what he says."

The next phone call came three days later. Over the years, when something even I find amazing happens, I will jokingly say, "As predicted," but in this case, Anita giddily quoted me. "As predicted, Karen. I can't believe it. The owners decided to sell. We are seeing the house and hopefully writing an offer this afternoon! Say a prayer for me, please."

A few hours later she called again. "Karen, it's official. I am practically speechless. When we walked into the house, there were Mexican pavers in the entry and a spiral staircase to the right, exactly like the other one! The doorknobs and fittings are exactly the same, only painted over, and it has the same master bedroom! It's just too weird! They are identical! Down to the last detail, only this one is much bigger and hasn't been redone! This is unbelievable. We love it!"

There was one last thing she needed to address, and I had to bring it up. "That is great news, honey! I am so happy for you. Did you find out about the fault under the kitchen yet?"

Her joy didn't waiver. "Not yet, but I told my broker to dig around for it, and after everything else, I'm sure it'll show up. We did write a full-price offer, though, and should know sometime tomorrow afternoon, and trust me, you'll hear from me."

The next time I heard from Anita she was practically hysterical. "I can't believe this is happening! The owners accepted our offer, but before we had a chance to sign the papers, some guy came along and offered $340,000! I thought you said the house was ours! What happened? Now they want way over the full asking price, and we can't do that. I can't believe we lost this house! How could this happen?"

Still certain this was their house, I said, "Please don't be upset. I know this is pretty unnerving, but I still see you buying that house. I promise."

"How, Karen? How is that going to happen? The guy has ten days to come up with a $90,000 down payment, and we can't pay $340,000 for that house! Now I have to start looking all over again!"

I was positive this was just a bump in the road, to give them some much-needed time. "He will never come up with that money, Anita, and please don't bother looking for another house, because you're moving into this one. Just start packing, because it will be a very quick escrow, and don't forget to have them look for the fault under the kitchen. I know you're hysterical right now, but they need to keep doing title searches while you're packing."

She was completely disheartened. They had sold their townhouse in one day and were now playing beat-the-clock to find a house and get out.

I couldn't believe the owners had accepted their offer and then changed their minds. I couldn't help feeling terrible for my friends.

Anita was practically inconsolable over what I knew was but a temporary turn of events. All I could do was reassure her that the house was hers, and urge her again to start packing.

There was nothing for anyone to do at this point except wait for the clock to tick down on the mystery buyer's down payment. The roller coaster ride over their purchase of this house had become unbearable, even for me. I knew in my soul this was their house. Unfortunately, I couldn't magically instill my certainty of their future in them.

Anita chose to ignore my advice about packing, and continued looking at other houses. Now she was hysterical and running herself crazy and, as I knew she would, found nothing.

On the morning of the tenth day, the roller coaster ride finally slowed to a glide. "I know I keep saying the same thing to you, but I can't believe how crazy this is, Karen! I just got off the phone with my broker, and the man can't come up with the down payment; the house fell out of escrow! Do you still see us in this house? What about the price? I can't meet that price."

I was emotionally exhausted but happy for them, all at the same time. "That's great, and absolutely yes! I have always seen you in this house. I keep harping on this, but what happened with the title searches? When they find the cloud on the title, the price will come down to $278,000. Where are they on this?"

Anita was breathless now. "Oh my God, I can't believe I forgot to tell you: they found it! My broker was beginning to think I was crazy, because I kept pushing him, even while I was looking at other houses. I have no idea how they found it, but it did take four searches for them to find the cloud on the title. You were right, the fault runs right underneath the kitchen. What should I do?"

Now that all the pieces fit neatly together in my mind, I became very calm. "Tell your broker to use the fault report to negotiate the price. They knew it was there all along and chose not to disclose it. Shame on them. Now get off the phone with me and call him right now. I know you still think I'm crazy, but congratulations on your new home."

Within a couple of hours, the long, drawn-out drama over the house was finished. Not only did the truth about the fault show up rather mysteriously, but the soil reports, complete with all the information Anita needed to cost out the necessary repairs, also magically appeared along with it. The owners came forward pretty quickly, suddenly flexible and willing to negotiate the price. The escrow was a short one, and before we all knew it, the hysteria had faded and Anita and her husband moved into their $278,000 home on Tareco Drive. The repairs on the fault running under the kitchen began almost immediately, with the final bill totaling $70,000.

My heart was at peace for my friends. I had tried very hard, over the crazy weeks and during the dozens of hysterical phone calls, to share with her what I saw. I kept hoping that my certainty would somehow be contagious, and that she would know in her heart what I knew as fact. No matter how hard I tried to help her see her life through my eyes, I came to the realization that it was never going to happen. It was simply impossible.

In thousands of readings over the years, I have wished, if only for a moment, that people could see what I see, and feel what I feel. Not just by giving a reading but literally letting them see their life through my eyes.

I realize though that what I see with such clarity and detail, and the peace of mind I experience for a client in a reading, are, and will forever be, nontransferable.

9

A Texas Story

It was a strange place, Texas, and Houston had a life all its own. In September of 1979 the people were wild and the air humid and hot, sticking to you like steam on a mirror.

There was a peculiar undercurrent throughout Houston. I could feel the impatience in the air. When I arrived at the Houston airport, I should have known this was the beginning of an experience to remember.

The journalist's husband was there to greet me, but he had no idea who I was when I said "Hello" to him.

He ignored me for about fifteen minutes, until I walked right up to this short, conservatively dressed, bespectacled attorney and introduced myself.

He was shocked and more than a little embarrassed; he told me I looked too normal to be a psychic and thought that I had been trying to pick him up!

When I told him I was Karen Page, he looked me up and down, and, with a straight face, said he expected me to have a turban on and to come sweeping into the airport on a broom! Of course, since I looked like a "normal" person, he felt pretty foolish.

Anyway, we went to a restaurant and had a very pleasant dinner with his also completely taken-aback wife, Mary. She was warm, genuine, and lovely. She was about 5'5", painfully thin, and dressed in perfect polyester, with shoulder-length brown hair.

She did the interview for the newspaper over dinner, telling me she didn't usually do these kinds of stories, but since I was a psychic I probably already knew that. She usually wrote stories on all the beautiful homes around Houston.

She said this just seemed so, well, so, you know, "*different.*" She just had to give it a try, and besides, gee whiz! She had never met a real-life psychic before.

The interview went surprisingly well. She was really amazed by the fact that I led a pretty normal life. You know, I have to wash my dishes, clean out the kitty-litter box, have my car serviced, and brush my teeth every day.

There was an air of "Wow!" to the entire interview, but I loved it. They were genuinely nice people, right out of *Father Knows Best*. I tried to help them stop thinking I was going to levitate the table during or after dinner, but to this day I think they were more surprised that I didn't.

The newspaper article came out the following Sunday, unleashing the most unbelievable response. The paper had to put on extra switchboard operators to handle the calls and give out my phone number. My phone rang incessantly; from the crack of dawn into the wee hours of the night, I booked appointments.

I love my work, so I was happy as a lark and thrilled to be that openly accepted in the Bible Belt of America.

One day a rather large, six-foot-tall, dark-haired lady came for a reading. During the course of her session, I discovered she was a police officer with the Houston Police Department, homicide division. She asked me rather pointedly if I ever worked with the police, and I told her yes. Without much detail, she enlisted my talents to help the Houston Police Department with a rather perplexing murder case they were trying to solve.

I was staying in a condo complex owned by a client of mine. The complex was brand-new. There were three buildings in a U-shape, with a total of seventy-six units. I was in the front building in the lower center unit. I found out the building wasn't quite finished and that only three units were occupied, one in each building.

There was a caretaker on the premises, whom I never saw, and a very lovely lesbian couple, Carol and Lori, who worked for my client. They were quite helpful to me during my adjustment to the new building. I had been staying in another condo complex, also owned by my client, until this unit was ready for me.

It took about three weeks to get the condo finished, and have me moved in and settled. I was booked solid, working sixteen- to eighteen-hour days without any breaks.

The girls had become my little guardian angels. They helped me move in and would bring me lunch and dinner whenever I finished working every day.

One day they took me for Chinese food to meet their friend Mr. Lee. He was quite a character. I had the great joy of watching him dissect a chicken in ten seconds flat, skin and all. After giving me the once-over, he decided he liked me. I was the genuine article and not some gypsy from outer space.

We went there often, and after Mr. Lee got to know me, he started having very vivid dreams about me that really disturbed him. He decided not to say anything about them for quite a while, until things *really* got weird, and by then he felt that he had no other choice.

The police detective and her captain called for an appointment one day, not too long after I had moved to the new unit.

I was booked up from morning until night, and had to make time to spend with my clients who brought me to Texas. Having those famous Sunday-afternoon barbecues with the governor of Texas and the owner of the Houston Oilers football team was also part of my job.

I had to juggle things around a bit not to sound too weird to these Texas detectives, so the appointment was set for about a week later, in the evening. I had planned to be finished with my readings by eight or nine that particular evening, and figured I could give them a couple of hours then.

I didn't think too much about the appointment with the detectives until I finished working one evening, about midnight, and decided to walk down the street to Denny's and get a bite to eat. The waitress asked if I was planning to eat by myself, and when I told her yes, she looked very surprised. Then she asked me if I had parked my car in the lot, and I told her I had walked. This time she almost fainted.

I didn't understand her concern, or her reaction, so I asked why she was so shocked. She told me she thought I was very brave to go out by myself, particularly at night, with this guy running around on the loose cutting up women.

Well, of course I thought she must be referring to some other part of Texas, and Texas, as we all know, is a very big place, so I never felt threatened or scared. I just thought she was overreacting to newspaper headlines exploiting some phantom in the night.

If I had known at that moment that grisly dissections of women were going on not five or six blocks from where I sat comfortably munching my cheeseburger, and that in a few short days I would know, up close and personally, more than I ever wanted to know about human lunacy, I probably would never have stepped foot out of my condo again, even if I starved from that day forward.

What I found out shortly after that little outing in Houston would chill the stoutest of hearts and make every young woman, from twenty to forty, never leave her home or answer her door for anyone, for any reason, ever again. Had I known, I would have thought twice about this innocent request to help the police. But ignorance is bliss, and what did I know from someone cutting up people like frogs?

Without another thought, I went right back to my eighteen-hour-a-day schedule of readings, and when the day came to see the police about this case, I was no more well informed than I had been that evening at Denny's.

I was even less prepared when the detectives arrived for their appointment. They were accompanied by other detectives lugging several banker boxes and stacks of files being carried like schoolbooks, from hip to shoulder. I asked them what all of this was, telling them it wasn't necessary to bring me everything they had ever done on this case. They said that they hoped it would help me give them a clue as to what the hell was going on with this monster.

I was talking to the female detective when I asked the captain if he had brought a picture of the victim. What he did after that, I don't know if I will ever understand. From across the room I watched him take a stack of photos out of one of the boxes. He meticulously lined them up, side by side, until they covered the top of my coffee table. I walked over to find that the pictures he had so carefully laid out were the actual crime scene photos of a decapitated woman's torso splayed out on a bed. There was no blood, and no head in sight.

I backed away from them, horrified, asking him what he thought he was doing. From the moment he walked in, the few words he had spoken to me had been rather short and dismissive, and I realized that he resented coming to see a psychic for help on his murder case. He had been a detective for many years and didn't want my help. As far as he was concerned, I was just some kook from California. Since he didn't know me, or what to expect, he was going to shock me with grisly crime-scene pictures. Sarcastically, he said, "Well, you told me to bring you a picture of the victim. Isn't this what you wanted?"

I was visibly shaken but tried to restrain myself. "No, this isn't what I wanted. Don't you have any pictures of the victim when she was alive? Or maybe one of her smiling with her dog?"

His answer was another sarcastic "No."

So this was what I had to work with, a tabletop covered with murder-scene pictures. Even without the help of their captain, they hoped I could come up with *something*, as they were at their wit's end with this senseless, horrifying set of circumstances. Not only were they frustrated, with no idea where to start, but they were embarrassed in the eyes of the Houston community in their apparent inability to come up with even the slightest direction in which to begin.

To add insult to injury, they had two identical murders, two weeks apart, both on a Thursday night. They had occurred in the same building, one floor apart. The victims not only lived in the same apartment on different floors, but they also knew each other. The HPD was looking pretty inept, so in spite of their captain, they were quite desperate for some help by the time they rang my doorbell that evening.

I tried to get to the core of this case from the moment they walked in. I tried not to clutter my mind, or their minds, with any of the useless information their officers had gathered while going on wild goose chases all over Texas.

We started with stacks of forensic lab photos of body parts—stacks and stacks of Polaroids taken at the scene. All I needed was one from each crime, but the police were intent on filling the top of my coffee table with multiple shots from every angle, figuring lots of these photos would help.

I finally got them to understand that what I really needed to help them was one plain, not fancy, picture of each victim. Excuse the morbid pun, but since they did not have a headshot available to give me, I would just work with one of the torso shots they brought, and there were definitely plenty to choose from.

I started telling them the reason and makeup of the crime—that this was a sex-related crime, and the murderer knew his victims but would not know the next one.

I proceeded to tell them what the next victim would be like: she would have red hair; be quite petite; would have been in Texas for a very short time, about six weeks; and would be from Florida. I told them that she had a boyfriend already, and that this crime would be different. It would occur outside, not in the girl's apartment. I also knew what day they could expect it. Six days from that very evening.

I told them what motivated the killings and how the murderer selected and approached his victims, gained their trust, *and* gained entry to their apartments.

I told them he was not from the Houston area originally and that they would find the first victim's head buried beneath the rear steps of his mother's home. His mother lived in a yellow house with a large backyard area and a front and rear porch, with a church nearby. I also told them that I saw the killer in a white coat, that he worked in a medical facility in Houston and had access to medical tools and equipment.

I knew he had a total and complete split personality. He would commit one of these murders, and later go have breakfast at the same diner he always went to and sit at the counter reading about the murder in the paper, commenting on what kind of a terrible person would do something like this. This was all before I gave them his physical description. I told them he was over six feet tall with short blond hair. He wore glasses and was sort of preppie-looking, in a nerdy sort of way. They would find that he had a history of mental illness and had started cutting up animals as a small child. I also knew that his current obsession with dissecting human beings appeared to be a point of graduating to a higher form for him. We are talking really sick. I knew that he had a criminal record, and if they had pictures of the convicted sex offenders in the Houston area, I would like to see them. Well, of course they had pictures, about forty or so, and they just happened to have them with them.

As they dug around searching for this stack of photographs, they informed me that they had already spoken to most of these guys, still had nothing to go on, and were completely and totally at a loss.

They clearly didn't know what they were dealing with, and didn't even know if these guys were in the area at the times of the murders, since they were *just* convicted sex offenders and *not* murderers. That little differentiation makes a big difference when dealing with something like this. They stated they had pictures of forty or so guys who were *only* convicted sex offenders, and in the eyes of the law they were *not*, I repeat *not*, heinous sex murderers.

We went back and forth on this point for several minutes while they fumbled around with their files. When they finally produced the requested stack of pictures, I flipped through them relatively quickly and, much to their surprise, about halfway through I tossed a picture across the table at them and said, "This is your guy."

They looked stunned, and muttered something along the lines of "Just like that?"

I trudged forward, urging them to check into his background, certain they would find a rather detailed history of mental disturbance from his childhood onward. I warned them that they would find him to be the only one of the lot that would pass a lie detector test, hands down. From my vantage point, he gave the word *schizophrenic* a whole new meaning. The detective told me he was afraid to go to this guy's house and open the refrigerator, afraid of what he might find.

After my clear and certain identification of their elusive murderer, they just sat there, continuing to ask me if I was sure, because to them, he was *only* a sex offender, with no prior history of murder. I looked at them, practically begging them to check out the information I had given them. If I was wrong, they could call me *pisher*, but if the information I had given them was correct, then go get him. I also knew something else. Unfortunately, it would take one more brutal murder before they could nail him. If they worked quickly, it would only be one more. Not a dozen more.

Thinking I had done my job, I told them to feel free to call me if there was anything else I could assist them with. They assured me they would let me know what was going on. We said our goodbyes, and I went into the kitchen to make myself a cup of very strong, black coffee.

Every time I work on a murder case like this, it makes me think about the twisted illness of human nature. What could possibly cause such a snap in someone's mind?

I didn't hear from them for about a week, and then I read the newspaper. The redheaded girl from Florida was front-page news. As predicted.

My phone rang with a request from the police captain to come by and talk to me again. I stood by my word, shuddered, and said yes. We set a date and they showed up as scheduled. Again, I was not prepared for their proposition. They had indeed checked out the facts against my feelings, and clearly began to see there just might be something to this "spooky psychic stuff."

The murder of the Florida girl really gave them a spin. They realized they had better act quickly, or who would be next?

Indeed, the man I had picked from the photographs was from outside Houston. He was from a small town, and his mother lived in a yellow house with a large backyard and a front and rear porch, just as I had described. The most important parts were yet to come. They found out that he did work in a medical facility, and there absolutely was a history of mental disturbance. He had been treated as a child, at a mental facility, for cutting up small animals.

What they requested of me during this second meeting was so shocking and ridiculous, I was certain they were joking.

I was that same psychic from Los Angeles whom they had treated like a carnival sideshow attraction. Their captain had been rude to me; they argued with me about everything I said; and now they wanted me, whom they didn't believe to begin with, to go talk to this guy!

They reasoned that obviously, because of my strange gift to see and know things, I could get through to him and get him to talk.

I didn't have the slightest desire to find out what they might have been thinking, trying to put me in the sights of this lunatic. I suggested they get a veterinarian to see him, since he had such an obvious interest in animals. However, they failed to see the humor in my train of thought, as they found themselves once again at a loss and could not get me to cooperate by becoming their sacrificial lamb. I tried to reason with them. I explained to them that his knowing I was the one who pinpointed him as the blade-wielding fruit loop of Texas was of no benefit to their case. But it did place me in considerable danger.

They did not share my point of view, but I was adamant about not facing this guy, whether they could see the situation through my eyes or not. They pleaded with me to think about it, so I told them rather halfheartedly that I would. But the answer was still no, and I knew it wouldn't change. They were very disappointed when they left, asking me to stay in touch.

I tried very hard to put this crazy episode behind me and go back to my regular grind, but within a few days of their last visit, the strangest set of circumstances started to overtake my very existence.

I was suddenly faced with the kind of terror I have never known in my life. It began with a restlessness that I couldn't shake. I was tossing and turning every night. I felt like someone was watching me. I double-locked the front door and began drawing the drapes. I booked myself from early morning to midnight, just so I wouldn't be alone. I couldn't eat, and for me that was a serious sign. I couldn't sleep, jumping up with a start, out of some unknown fear inside me. I turned on every light in my condo unit and secured every window. I was terrified for my life, and I didn't know why.

A friend from California called to ask if I was okay. He asked me to analyze a dream that he'd had the night before. He told me he dreamt of a large brick barbecue that had been burnt and charred on the chimney. In the same dream he said he had seen himself with a thin red line around his neck—when the truth was that it was *me* in his dream, and I had the thin red line around my neck, but he was too afraid to tell me. He thought by calling to say hi, he could check up on me without scaring me half to death by telling me the truth.

What he didn't know was that I was living in the grip of unspeakable fear every day. If he had told me the truth about my presence in his dream, I would have been able to decipher my fear as being very real and very near. The days and nights began running into one another for me. I was losing weight like crazy, had dark circles under my eyes, and was certain I kept hearing someone walking around in the empty, unfinished unit above my head— and the worst part of it all was that I was dealing with this invisible horror alone.

I asked my host, for safety's sake, to replace the glass doors to the patio with bulletproof glass and to black out all the windows. I wanted to make sure no one could look into my condo. I knew that I was being stalked, but because it was me, and not someone else, I couldn't get a clear handle on it.

I confided my fears to Carol and Lori, who did everything possible to calm me down, short of babysitting me twenty-four hours a day. I called my friend Tracy and asked her to come help me in Houston. I flew her down the very next day, but not before I had Lori acquire a .357 Magnum and a can of mace for me. Her brother was the head of a local police department, so these requests were easily filled. They knew that I was alone and had been working on this violent murder case, not to mention that I was noticeably freaked out over something they could not begin to understand.

These murders were terrifying the city, and since I was in such close proximity, both physically and psychically, Carol and Lori voiced the fear that maybe, just maybe, the police had let the cat out of the bag. I should have some protection. Whatever this mysterious terror was, it had me pacing the floors every night, clutching my prayer book to my chest. With every day that passed, my spiritual protection became my only hope.

Carol and Lori were completely stymied in their efforts to help me. They kept hoping the HPD would pick this man up, so I could calm down and get some sleep. I looked like a woman going over the edge.

I remember looking at myself in the mirror one night, knowing so clearly I was going to die soon. Someone or something was trying to kill me. I just couldn't see what "it" was.

I met my friend Tracy at the Houston airport. My right hand was plunged inside my purse, clutching the trigger of a gun. My left hand clasped, ready for action, the can of mace. I figured that whatever this was, if it came toward me, I at least had a chance. I felt like a commando in a jungle of faceless enemies, and one of them had my blood on their hands.

Tracy simply thought I was overworked and suffering from exhaustion. She couldn't feel the fear and thought I desperately needed a rest. She, Carol, and Lori all felt

I was on the verge of a nervous breakdown. But I knew I was on the verge of losing my life.

I kept Tracy up playing cards or watching television with me every night after I finished work. We talked about the most ridiculous things, because I would do almost anything not to be left alone.

Tracy asked me what I was so terrified of. She reasoned that "they," whoever my imaginary "they" was, could not get through the patio door, couldn't shoot me while I sat there giving readings, couldn't see into the condo from any of the windows, and with three deadbolts on the front door, what in God's name did I think was going to happen? How did I think they were going to get in here to kill me?

I felt so broken looking at my friend. I started to cry and told her, "They are going to come right through the front door."

She asked me why she couldn't feel the threat. I told her that they didn't want her. They wanted to kill me. I was the one who had received so much publicity through the newspaper and television. I was highly visible and had become the "Toast of Houston." She was not the target...I was. I had been working with the police to catch people who committed horrible crimes. I clearly was the one being stalked, not her. She was safe. "They" would not touch her. Of this I was certain.

With every passing day, I was becoming more hysterical inside. I knew that if I stayed in Houston, I wouldn't be alive much longer. Texas would become my grave, if I didn't leave and go home.

How painfully aware I became of my dedication to my work. I could not reconcile my imminent death with abandoning all the people I had set appointments with. I couldn't seem to make the decision to leave them high and dry, and there were far too many appointments to call and cancel.

Since it looked like I wouldn't live to leave Texas, I really didn't know what to do. I asked God for the answer. It came to me very clearly, in a dream at the end of October. I lay down on my bed with almost every light in the condo on, and my ever-present prayer book clutched firmly to my chest.

I rested just long enough to stop pacing the two-bedroom condo for the millionth time, to give my weary, sleep-deprived body a break. I dozed off. In an instant there appeared a deeply treasured gift from my mother, a very unusual lapis lazuli watch, floating in space. The hands clearly said 11:10. The dream then flipped to a telephone number with an area code of 703, which I had never heard of, and my original phone number, from the first apartment I occupied in Texas. The phone number kept going around in the dream, to make certain I imprinted it on my subconscious.

I awoke with a start, ran into Tracy's darkened bedroom, sat down on the edge of her bed, and quietly awakened her from much-needed sleep. I recounted my dream to her and started to cry, begging her to find out where the area code belonged, if there was such an area code in existence.

She called information and was told it belonged to a "small town in Virginia." I knew in my soul that this was the answer, but the answer to what, I didn't know. I didn't know anyone from a small town in Virginia, and at the time I didn't understand the importance of 11:10 on my watch. I would come to realize that it didn't represent a time, but actually a date, November 10th, which was a little more than a week away.

I asked Tracy to take me home to California, because if I didn't leave Houston I was going to die soon. In her exhausted stupor she tried to reason with me, saying I was just tired and that she couldn't take me home because I was booked for six months solid and had commitments to keep. She was sure it was just my lack of sleep talking.

As I sat there looking at her trying to reassure me, my shoulders slumped forward. I mumbled that I was going to die, closed my eyes, and floated out of my body. I was hovering about six inches to the left of where my body sat.

Tracy completely freaked out, jumping up from the bed and violently shaking my arm to bring me back. Nervously, she said, "Okay, okay, when do you want to leave?"

Very quietly, I said, "Now."

She shrieked at me that it was three o'clock in the morning! How was she supposed to get us out of there now? Finally relenting, she told me she would see what she could arrange.

What I needed to live another day was the first plane out of Houston. There was so much confusion from that moment on. Tracy made phone calls fast and furiously, trying to get us on almost any nonstop flight to L.A. that even came near the Houston airport.

I called Carol and Lori and informed them that we were leaving, asking them for a ride to the airport, and to please come and help. They said they were on their way.

Mr. Lee had told them about having some very disturbing dreams about me, and he finally told them that he felt I was in danger, even though he didn't know from what. He told them about all of the dreams, from the beginning. Being a very superstitious man, he was gravely concerned when his dreams involved my soul floating down the street after emerging from a sewer drainpipe. This was the dream that finally scared him into picking up the phone.

Tracy found us a flight leaving at 11:30 a.m. I prepaid the tickets so there would be no fuss or wasted time at the airport.

I silently prayed we could just get on the plane and leave this Godforsaken place. We began running around, throwing things into bags from every room, leaving about half of my things for the killer. I didn't care, I just wanted out of this Hell.

Carol and Lori came rushing into the condo. If I were not so hysterical at the time, I probably would have fallen on the floor laughing at this ridiculous scene. They dragged in a huge shopping bag and started pulling things out that resembled crosses and crucifixes, of every conceivable shape and size.

Just the thought of them bringing in these huge crosses, and not to forget the crucifix that Carol's mother had given to her for me, was the funniest thing I could possibly imagine. I just stopped and stood there, staring at the two of them running through the condo, propping these crosses against anything that would hold them, in every room, including the bathroom.

I started yelling, "What the Hell are you doing? I'm not being stalked by a vampire!" But to no avail. Carol kept pulling crosses out of the bag. I had to stop this right now! I was leaving Texas immediately, and no amount of crosses in the world were going to stop me.

To this day, I wonder where they got so many of them on such short notice, along with all the other strange and bizarre things they pulled out of that bag.

If I didn't have a deep and abiding faith in God as the foundation of my life, I would have been dead a long time ago, but the crosses they were so intent on surrounding me with were clearly not what I had in mind. I was much more concerned with not wasting any more precious time getting to the airport. I returned the gun and mace to Carol, lugged the bags out to the car, and off we went.

We arrived in plenty of time, but with that kind of energy operating in a person's life, there will be obstacles placed in front of them at every turn. I got in line to pick up our prepaid tickets, but without giving any reason at all, the clerk refused to issue them to me. She made us wait three and a half hours for the next flight to L.A.

Sitting in the coffee shop, Tracy asked me if I felt any better. I told her not until my feet were on the ground in L.A. would I be okay. She told me I needed a long rest, and spoke to me like I was being taken away to a sanitarium.

I was very nervous sitting in the airport and kept looking over my shoulder. I wouldn't even go to the bathroom, for fear of not coming out again.

When we finally boarded the plane, I prayed for take-off. I looked sick and exhausted, like I was slipping over the edge. The desperation to save my life had finally reached its last steps.

I slumped into a nervous dozing, only to be startled awake by the pattern of the airplane's engines. I was so tight with fear from all of the weird events over the past two months. I finally caved in to the internal silence, saying quiet prayers of protection to get us home unharmed.

I wanted to see my mother's face and share a cup of coffee with her in my big, yellow country kitchen. I desperately needed to feel safe. It had been a long time since I felt warm and whole. I wasn't used to terror. It was a remote and unfamiliar emotion for me, touching the depths of my soul.

How do you explain something that you can't understand yourself? You search your memories for hidden enemies, but draw a blank. You reason with life, and come to truly know the foundations of your faith. You test the monuments to immortality that we, as human beings, secretly arm ourselves with every day. How painfully aware I became of life's fragile nature. How precious time became. My priorities came sharply into focus; there was no time to waste. It was too precious, and too much joy was being ripped from the fibers of my fragile soul. How fervently I prayed for time.

When we finally arrived home, I was so exhausted that all I could be was quiet and grateful.

On this Wednesday evening, I wanted to look into my mother's eyes, and just feel safe. To be surrounded by what was familiar and welcome. I listened for the quiet to return to my soul, but it was a very long time in coming.

I had put the Houston case in some dark corner of my mind. I quietly promised myself that if I ever again worked with any police department, anywhere, I would be placed in a more protected set of circumstances. Not just cast aside. If in fact this was what had set me up for the kill, I vowed never to allow myself to be treated like a handi-wipe again. The price was too high. I was not willing to sacrifice my life, and all of my dreams, to be stalked by some crazed lunatic with an obsession to take up carving.

The next couple of days were thankfully uneventful. I stuck close to home, and when the phone rang on Friday night, with Carol's voice on the other end, I was grateful again to be home in L.A.

She asked me how I was, but sounded a little strained when asking if I finally felt safe. She told me that she finally understood everything now. Warily, she proceeded to ask me the name of the town represented by the 703 area code in my dream. I told her, "It was a small town in Virginia. Why?"

She said a rather odd thing occurred on the day I left Houston. She and Lori had gone back to clean up my condo, but before going into mine, they decided to check the condo upstairs from me. What they found freaked both of them out, and now they knew that I was not crazy. Someone *had* been spending a lot of time in that empty unit. They found old candy wrappers, cigarette butts everywhere, and, most frightening of all, numerous newspaper clippings about me scattered about the floor and taped in a cross pattern on the wall.

They immediately went looking for the caretaker, only to find that he had cleared out while they were taking me to the airport. They went to their files to check his record, and discovered he was from a small town in Virginia.

Carol, not one to believe in coincidence, decided something was very strange about all of this and called Lori's brother. She asked him to do a background check on this guy. What they got back unnerved them beyond words. He'd had a police record in Virginia and was in Houston after having escaped from jail.

The charges against him were attempted murder.

I sat frozen on the other end of the line. Her next words chilled my heart: "The woman he tried to murder was a psychic."

Through my tears I whispered, "With his hands."

She quietly replied, "Yes, he tried to strangle her."

Carol confirmed that he had virtually vanished into thin air.

I cried and cried. What could I do but wonder if he was on his way to California?

I don't know if they ever caught the serial killer in Houston, but the Karen Page stalker haunted me for many, many years. It took almost a year for me to feel safe again. I don't look over my shoulder or carry a .357 Magnum in my purse anymore, but as I sit here many years after the fact, the terror is still too easy to recall.

And I wonder if maybe someday I will have another dream.

10

Unwelcome Home

On a sunny afternoon in 1972, I inched up a narrow driveway on Fountain Avenue. I stepped out, walking across the lawn to get a better view of the house my friend Wally had moved into the week before.

It was a lovely Craftsman-style home, set back from the street and featuring large windows on either side of the entrance. Large, round columns anchored a wide porch running the width of the house. We had lunch plans, but Wally wanted to give me the twenty-five-cent tour before we took off.

He stood smiling in the doorway, beckoning me in. I crossed the threshold into a large, rectangular living room with two old-fashioned windows flanking a big brick fireplace on the far-left wall.

I was drawn into the energy and instantly loved this house. It was obvious to me that it had been lovingly cared for, and though it wasn't a glamorous house, it really felt like "Old Hollywood." Before taking another step I said, "Wally, if you ever decide to move out of here, please call me first. I would love to rent this house."

Surprised by my comment, he smiled nervously, muttering, "Don't think I'm movin' any time soon, Karen," and turned to finish giving me the tour.

To the right was a beautiful sunroom filled with natural light from the surrounding windows. I followed Wally's lead along gleaming wood floors, passing through a formal dining room with six tall French windows lining the outer wall.

We entered a big, old-fashioned kitchen. Without a word, Wally crossed over to lean against the counter as I moved to stand in the center of the marble linoleum floor. Wally covered his mouth, smiling, watching as I slowly turned around to take it all in.

The more I looked around, the more I realized how sophisticated this old-fashioned kitchen really was. It was wonderful, but in a really odd sort of way. In spite of this being an old Craftsman home in the heart of Hollywood, the kitchen just "looked" old, and was the size of a catering kitchen in a hotel. It had everything my cook's heart could ever want: double ovens, a professional six-burner Wolf range, an oversized sink, wraparound counters and cabinets, and a huge refrigerator and freezer.

I have always believed that "love lives" in the kitchen of a house, and *this* kitchen spoke directly to my heart. From the time I moved into my first apartment, I have entertained in my home and had always done all the cooking myself, no matter how many people were coming. I have always enjoyed hosting Thanksgiving, holiday, and birthday celebrations, as well as random dinner parties throughout the year, so this kitchen was a dream.

As I wandered from appliance to cabinet, looking at everything, Wally never moved from his perch. I stepped through a doorway at the far end of the kitchen to find another hidden jewel, a totally equipped service porch with a full-sized washer and dryer, shelving, more cabinets, and a large, very deep sink.

During all of my "Wow!"s and ongoing proclamations of "What a *great* house!" Wally just watched me, never uttering a word.

He had spent a lot of time in my kitchen over the years and knew how much I love to cook, so when we finally left this funny, odd, and amazing kitchen, he reminded me once again, "You know I just moved in, Karen, so please don't start packing yet. I'm planning to be here awhile."

I didn't know what had come over me since I walked in the front door. I had no connection to this house, nor did I have any intention or interest in moving anywhere at that time, and I had never even considered living in this area. All of it was a bit surreal and completely out of character for me. My logic had apparently flown right out the window when it came to anything about this peculiar little house on Fountain.

From the moment I walked through the front door, I felt like I had been hypnotized by the energy in this house. I knew it didn't make any sense, but I felt that I was *supposed* to be in this house. I could "see" myself living there, not in some sort of wishful thinking way, but in a certain and knowing way.

Though I had no idea how my living in this house would ever come about, I knew in my heart that I *would*, even though Wally had just moved in. I couldn't seem to stop myself. "Oh, I didn't mean now, but when and if you do move again, please call me. I would rent this house in a heartbeat."

We were done with the tour, and out the front door we went, chattering all through lunch. Wally was a lovely, soft-spoken guy, and we had been friends from the time I started giving readings. We saw each other socially throughout the years, but when a sweep of life-changing events started blowing through his life, we started seeing each other more frequently.

The gale-force winds of change lasted almost a year for Wally, and during that difficult period we started having what I called "therapy lunches" around Los Angeles. He was finally ready to begin putting his life back together, and moving into the house on Fountain Avenue was the first step.

He had been married to a well-known actress for several years. Though she was many years older than Wally, it never appeared to be an issue, and their marriage seemed loving and close. Everything was fine between them. Until one day it wasn't, and suddenly, without warning, their outwardly happy marriage was simply over.

Wally was like a brother to me, and though his marriage appeared to be fine to the outside world, I had looked at it through very different eyes. I had always felt that she "cared" about him, but in their life together, she treated him like a pet, or her "boy toy." It was also clear to me from the beginning that he never knew that, because he had truly loved her.

The rapid disintegration of their life together hadn't surprised me, but it turned Wally's life upside down. From one day to the next, it was over. There was no conversation, no healing possible. Out of nowhere, she slammed the door shut on their marriage. Overnight he was pushed out of her life, and out of the life they had shared. He had been lost, and this move was a beginning.

Wally was in a playful mood over lunch, teasing me about my funny reaction to his house and my special love affair with the kitchen. He reminded me that he never got around to showing me the layout of the bedrooms or the old-fashioned pedestal sink in the bathroom.

I laughed and said that I thought the kitchen *was* the whole house. I talked about how drawn I was to the house, and how unusual the energy in it felt. I told him that as far as I was concerned, after visiting the kitchen I didn't need to see the rest of the house.

For several weeks, even though we continued to meet occasionally for one of our "therapy lunches," I hadn't been back to the house. On one of our planned lunch days, Wally called to say he "had something to do and couldn't make it today," casually adding, "By the way, Karen, were you serious about wanting to rent the house?"

My heart started racing, sure that he was kidding. "You mean your house? Absolutely! Why, are you moving?"

He was trying to sound casual, like what he was about to tell me was an everyday occurrence. "Well, yeah, I'm moving into one of the apartments next door. Actually, I'm moving this afternoon. That's why I can't make lunch today." He paused to take a deep breath. "So, were you serious? Do you want to rent the house?"

All of a sudden, a mixture of shock and that weird hypnotic feeling I had experienced in the house overcame me. My logical mind, refusing to believe him, still needed to be convinced, or at least have him laugh and tell me he was setting me up, just to see my reaction.

The tone in his voice was serious, so I was completely confused and more than a little freaked out. He was so matter-of-fact about moving again that I still wasn't sure if he was telling me the truth.

My internal freakout continued. "What do you mean today?! Are you kidding? You just moved in six weeks ago! I mean, I love the house, so yes, I was serious, but you're not really moving today, are you?"

He didn't laugh. "Yup, I am. Pretty funny, huh? I can hardly believe it myself, but I am, and Karen, it's not like I'm going anywhere. I'll be right next door. So do you want the house?" I finally believed him.

I completely ignored my gut feelings and the incessant screaming in my mind, along with every other obvious sign to run in the other direction. Foolishly leaving my freaked-out suspicions about his sudden move unchecked, I never even bothered to ask him, "Why?"

I went running, skipping, and leaping headlong into the move. "Wow! Okay, if you're really moving? I'd love to rent the house, but have you talked to the landlord yet? And, please, if he says okay, don't forget to tell him that my mother will be living with me."

His voice was calmer now, saying he wanted to ask me if I was serious first, but would speak with the landlord and call me later that afternoon. His "later" wound up being less than ten minutes.

It appeared to be so easy, as though it was "meant to be." He said the landlord was delighted that I wanted the house, and told Wally to just give me the keys. He would stop by to meet my mother and me after we moved in.

I couldn't have known that, from the moment the word "Yes" fell from my lips in response to Wally's question, my life would be forever changed. That one simple word set in motion a series of events with life-altering consequences and profound lessons. For my mother and for me, nothing would ever be the same again.

As I switched into "autopilot" mode, my days became consumed with packing, utility companies, and movers, and—the most important part for me—making sure that my clients could find me. I still marvel at the fact that my mother and I were 100 percent organized, packed, and being moved in only two weeks!

I think moving day for everyone can be pretty crazy, no matter how organized and prepared you are. This moving day brought the usual crazy energy, along with a few really strange surprises by the end of the day.

I wanted my mother to be happy in our new home. Though I was sure she would love the kitchen, the rest of the house was a total mystery for both of us. By getting there before the movers and utility technicians arrived, we could take the rest of the house tour together, the one that I had missed the first time around.

As the move unfolded, I realized that I was completely unable to stop my illogical connection to this house. I could hardly believe that Wally was standing here in front of me, very nervously handing me the keys to my new home. The home I was moving my mother into, the home that I had rented over the phone without really seeing.

It was surprising, but we were definitely *here*; the keys were definitely *real*; and we definitely *were* about to move into a house that, as far as I knew, stopped at the kitchen. I had no idea what the bathroom looked like, or if the bedrooms were even big enough for our furniture; and as crazy as it sounds, none of that seemed to matter as my hand closed around the keys.

Wally's behavior that day was just weird, like he was going to jump out of his skin. I invited him in, but he turned and was sprinting up the stairs to his apartment by the time the words "No thanks" came out of his mouth.

At any other time, I would have asked him what was wrong, why he had been behaving so strangely. The truth is, he never told me anything, nor did I ever ask. I don't think I was supposed to know, because if I had known the source of Wally's irrational behavior, I promise you I would have made a very different choice.

It was a perfect day to move: the sun was shining and the air was crisp. We were both in a very happy mood, looking forward to this move. God bless the spirit of my wonderful mother; she didn't give it a second thought that I had only seen the front rooms of the house. She thought it was great, whatever it was, and looked at it as us embarking on a shared adventure.

My mother stood behind me as I slipped the key in the lock, crossing the threshold of our lovely home, without the slightest idea of the terrifying world we were stepping into.

I stepped aside as my mother checked out the front rooms, and as I had hoped, she loved them. Moving across to the doorway into the first bedroom, the real adventure was about to begin.

We were grateful to find that there was plenty of room for my bedroom furniture, and a very large closet. My mother decided this would be my room, and she would take the bedroom at the back of the house.

We continued into a square-shaped hallway between the two bedrooms. All of the doors in the hallway were open, except one. I peeked around one to discover a floor-to-ceiling linen closet, tucked away next to a connecting door leading back into the kitchen. The remaining open door led into a pristine, white-and-black-tiled bathroom.

While exploring the bathroom, my mother joked about what secrets we might find hidden behind the closed door to her "boudoir." We turned left out of the bathroom, standing in front of the closed door. Taking a deep breath, I gripped the doorknob, slowly pushing open the "boudoir" door.

I took one step and knew that my mother was never sleeping a night in this room. I couldn't move. Though the window shades were up to welcome this bright sunny day, not a sliver of light or warmth came through the windows of this room.

Unknowingly, I had stepped into the icy gray haze that filled every corner of the space; with a deep sense of dread, I realized that nothing could penetrate the "dead cold" enveloping this room.

Poking her head around, my mother attempted to get past me, only to jerk back instinctively from the shocking cold. Visibly shaken, she practically jumped back into the hallway, as I tried to catch my breath.

Someone had died in that room, and their energy was still there, hanging in the air. Forcing myself, I slowly backed out, firmly closing the door to this "room of death" for one last time. I stood silent trying to gather my thoughts, staring at the door in front of me. I needed to be calm for my mother.

As I didn't know who had died, or the history of the house, I couldn't help them leave, or help my mother understand what had just happened in that room. In an instant I knew why I'd felt hypnotized from the moment I stepped in the house.

I turned around, smiling, cheerfully leading my mother into the kitchen. "Well, you're definitely never sleeping in that room! Let's go look at the kitchen."

I think she was too freaked out to ever ask me what happened, so there became an unspoken agreement between us never to speak of it again. We never opened the door again, and from that day forward, it was as though that room simply didn't exist.

Everything else about the move went on as scheduled, and as the furniture was being delivered, we decided to turn the sunroom into a very lovely bedroom for my mother. I secretly hoped that the bedroom would be the only anomaly we would have to deal with, because we both loved the house. Though I was very conscious about the terrifying energy in the bedroom, the "creep factor" was quickly becoming a non-issue, seeming to fade a little with every box we unpacked.

Within the first week, a handyman took care of my mother's short list of things she needed done in the house for her peace of mind, including the installation of a deadbolt on the door between the kitchen and the service porch. We cheered as we checked the last thing off her list. We were finally done with the move and could really enjoy our new home.

For the first month or so, everything appeared to be pretty normal. I was busy giving readings, and we had a housewarming party, along with a couple of small dinner parties with friends. It was a quiet and peaceful period for us, and it felt like life had finally returned to normal.

One afternoon I went into the kitchen, only to find the door between the kitchen and the service porch standing wide open. That was the door we'd had a deadbolt lock installed on for security, so I thought that maybe my mother had forgotten to lock it; I would ask her about it when she got up from a nap. A few minutes later she wandered into the kitchen to join me. Although she was still sleepy, I asked her about the door being left open, and she said, "How could I have left the door open, sweetheart? You have the only key to the lock, remember?"

I dropped what I was doing, running to get my keys out of my purse. There it was. The one and only key to the deadbolt, hanging on my key ring, and it had been in my possession since the day the lock was installed. Now I was completely baffled. I went back to the kitchen with my keys, looking closely at the door to see that it had definitely been unlocked. I closed the door, locking it and unlocking it two or three times. I turned the doorknob, pulling on the door, but it held fast. I know it seems like a small thing, but this was just crazy, and I knew for sure that the deadbolt didn't spontaneously unlock itself, so how in the world could this happen? Since we could find no logical explanation for the deadbolt being unlocked, we made it a habit to check the door every time we went near the kitchen.

One of the many jobs I held while building my practice was at Canter's Deli in Los Angeles. Because I gave readings during the day, I worked the eight in the evening to four in the morning shift, five or six days a week. Canter's wasn't very far from the house, so every night when I got home from work I would grab the newspaper and read it, sitting cross-legged on my antique four-poster bed, before I went to sleep.

One morning, as I quietly sat reading the paper, I started hearing footsteps. They were soft at first, so I tried to ignore them, but they became increasingly louder and more persistent, sounding as though there was someone walking around my bed. I was startled. I looked around the room, for what I don't know, because I couldn't see anyone, but there was definitely someone walking very closely around my bed. They were so close that I thought if I reached my arm out, I would touch them, but I was frozen in place and didn't move. For about ten minutes they continued walking back and forth, loud enough for me to hear the floorboards creaking under the measured footsteps. My mind was racing: who was this, and what did they want? All of a sudden the walking stopped just as suddenly as it had begun. I turned off the lights and lay in bed the entire night with my eyes wide open. My heart felt as if it was about to beat out of my chest as I tried to make sense of what had just happened.

My mother slept through the first time someone was walking around my bed, but the next time was on one of my days off, so it was earlier in the evening and she happened to be awake. I was reading in bed as the footsteps started; there was no question that someone wanted me to know they were there: the steps were loud, very close, and deliberate, causing the wood to creak incessantly as they strode around my bed. I sat up, softly calling out for my mother to please come into my bedroom.

The footsteps continued as my mother made her way across the living room. I didn't move a muscle, staring at the doorway in anticipation. I wanted her to hear them.

The moment she stepped into my room with "What's the matter, sweetheart?" the footsteps abruptly stopped. I looked around, attempting to explain the two incidents, but unless she could actually hear the footsteps herself, it sounded ridiculous, and was impossible for her to understand.

The footsteps had stopped, but I knew that the energy in the house had definitely changed. I simply wasn't ready to look at it, or deal with it, just yet. I started planning another dinner party, and wanted to set the food up buffet style in the dining room. There were six French windows lining the wall, and I wanted to have them open for the evening. When I went to open them several days before the party, I was surprised to find that every one of them had been nailed shut, from top to bottom, at three- or four-inch increments.

I ran into the owner the next afternoon and asked him if he could have the nails removed so I could open the windows in the dining room. He told me that they had been nailed shut for as many years as he could remember, and unfortunately he couldn't do it because the windows and the frames were so old, there was no way of removing all those nails without destroying the wood. I went back and looked at the window frames, and he was right. The nails had been hammered deep into the wood, with most of the nail heads below the surface of the frame—so that was the end of that, or so it seemed.

About four days after my conversation with the owner, my mother and I had run some errands to get ready for the party. We were gone about three hours and walked into the house laden down with groceries. As I stepped into the dining room, I noticed that every one of the windows was open, and open at exactly the same angle.

I dropped the bags inside the kitchen door, spinning around to look at the windows, but before I could walk around to them, I noticed the nails on the table. They weren't just strewn on the table; these rusted and bent three- or four-inch-long nails had been laid out in some odd pattern, as though they had purposely been placed in some kind of order, lined up next to each other like little soldiers. They were not only on the table, but the orderly line also flowed onto the chair, and finally onto the floor.

I stood there for a minute studying the bizarre layout. Finally pulling myself away, I went over to check the extent of the damage that had been done to the window frames. I touched the wood where the nails had been, and couldn't believe that there was no splintering; there were no gouge marks around the nail holes; and, though I knew it wasn't possible, there was no damage to the wood at all! The wood looked like the nails had been pulled straight out, leaving only the small holes they had been driven into! Mystified, I gathered up the bent and rusted nails, rubbing my fingers over the smooth wood one more time. I wanted to believe that the owner had come into the house and magically done this.

I was so happy to have them open that when I saw the owner again, I thanked him for taking the nails out of the window frames for me. He looked like he was going to faint, but didn't. Instead he stepped back, started fidgeting, and wouldn't look at me again. I waited for him to say something about the windows, but when he finally spoke, his voice was tight and he made it clear that he didn't want to talk about it. "I told you that I couldn't take those nails out, so I don't know what you're talking about, and I definitely had nothing to do with it. Have a good day, Karen." And with that, he turned and walked away.

From that day forward, the strange and unexplainable events in the house became increasingly more terrifying, started happening with much greater frequency, and were quite clearly directed at me.

Mother's Day was coming, and because my mother had been a florist for many years, I always went out of my way to have beautiful flower arrangements delivered to her on that special day. My friend David owned several flower shops, so he was my go-to guy for my mother. I asked him to do something spectacular for this particular holiday, and he definitely did. The arrangement was so big that when it was placed on the table in front of my mother's bed, it blocked the entire view into the living room. Many years earlier, my mother had given me a beautiful, turquoise glass ashtray from Sweden. It was quite large and very heavy, weighing about eight pounds. It had been a decorative piece on the table in my mother's room, so when the flowers were delivered, the ashtray was sort of tucked under the long flower stems, next to the base of the container holding them.

Late in the afternoon the day after the flowers were delivered, my mother was dozing in the sunroom and I was lying on the sofa, reading a book. It was very quiet in the house, and I must have been reading for about half an hour when, out of nowhere and just barely missing my head, my beautiful turquoise ashtray came whizzing past my head, and with a loud "boom" slammed into the fireplace, shattering into a million pieces. It was as though someone had picked it up and thrown it full force toward my head, like a baseball! I was terrified!

My mother jumped up, yelling, "What was that? Are you okay?"

I wasn't okay, but I couldn't even begin to tell my mother that someone, or something, had thrown my ashtray at me, and now it was in a million pieces all over the floor. Thankfully the flowers had blocked her view, so I went in to comfort her, trying desperately to keep my shaking to a minimum. I didn't want her coming into the living room to see what had happened, so I told her that I was a klutz and had dropped something. Making light of the noise, I kept her company until she had calmed down and I could get the dustpan and broom, and clean up the mess.

The series of incidents that had occurred up to this point I could almost ignore, because they were small in comparison and they hadn't been violent. This flying ashtray episode, though, was something entirely different. If their aim had been better, they would have killed me. I had to figure out what to do about this, whatever this was.

Three days after Mother's Day, I was taking my mother to a doctor's appointment, and on my way out of the house I remembered that I needed to take the flowers into the kitchen, to get rid of the few flowers that had died or were wilting and clean up the arrangement. We were running short on time, so I picked up the arrangement, took it into the kitchen, and set it on the counter to deal with when we got back. We were gone about two hours, and when we got home, I noticed the empty table and headed for the kitchen, with my mother following me.

When I got to the kitchen door, I couldn't believe my eyes. I could hardly breathe as I blocked the doorway, looking into the kitchen. I spun around, calmly asking my mother not to look in the kitchen, and to please go relax in the sunroom. I stepped into the kitchen to find every single one of the beautiful flowers that had been in the Mother's Day arrangement strewn all over the kitchen floor! Dead! The flowers were dry, gray, and brittle, with every bit of color drained out of them. They looked like they had been dead for a month! The now-empty container was the only thing left, and it sat alone on the counter, exactly where I had left it. A knot of fear began settling in my stomach as I collected the dead flowers from the floor. The menace in the house was escalating, and now I was worried that it was going to turn on my mother.

Though it appeared to have calmed down in the house, at least for a couple of weeks after the flower-killer episode, I was so on edge that sleep had become nearly impossible. I was sitting cross-legged on my bed one evening, reading the paper, when suddenly a familiar sound broke the quiet of the night. Someone was walking around my bed. The footsteps were louder than ever, and this time I was going to make sure that my mother heard them. I called out to her, once again asking her to please come to the door of my bedroom because I wanted her to hear something. I asked her not to come in, just to come to the door. In a minute, she was at my door, sleepily placing one hand on either side of the doorway, asking me, "What is it, sweetheart?"

I looked at my mother intensely, bringing my index finger up to my lips, signaling her to be quiet, softly saying, "Listen." I watched as she listened, her eyes widening with fear, as she finally realized that the sounds she was hearing were actual footsteps.

She didn't move from the doorway, now trying to make sense out of it. "Who's doing that?"

I was really freaking out inside, because this time the footsteps didn't stop when we spoke. I was trying very hard to remain calm, so I smiled at her, hoping she would remain calm, too. "I don't know, Mom. We haven't been formally introduced."

My mother abruptly turned out of the doorway, yelling, "I don't know what's going on, but I'm calling the police!"

I scrambled off the bed, trying desperately to stop her, but to no avail. The police were there in five minutes. My mother was very upset as she told them that someone had been walking around my bed. When they asked where I had been when it happened, I told them that I was sitting on the bed, reading. That just made them smile. One of the policemen put his hand on my shoulder, looked in my eyes, and asked, "Miss, have you been smoking any of those funny cigarettes? Or have you been drinking tonight?"

I was furious but polite. "No, officer, I don't do drugs and I don't drink, and I don't expect that you'd understand this situation, so I don't think you can help us, but thank you for coming anyway." They finally left, and were never called again.

I was completely petrified, and though we had only been living in the house for a little over three months at this point, I knew I was going to have to make arrangements for us to move. Unfortunately, the owner was out of the country and wouldn't be back for two weeks, so we had no other choice but to wait.

Also unfortunately, we were having a birthday party for a friend that had already been scheduled for a few days after our visit from the police. Since it was too late to cancel, we went ahead with it. The party was great until later in the evening. It started when one of our friends came into the kitchen with a terror-stricken look on her face. She leaned into me, and in a desperate whisper, said, "Something is wrong with your bathroom."

Walking through the kitchen, I crossed the hallway into the bathroom, where everything looked fine. I went into the living room to find out from her more detail about what had happened. She was standing with four other friends, all with the same terror-stricken looks on their faces. I knew this wasn't going to be good. Each one told me the same story: that when they went to use the bathroom, as they were sitting on the commode, it would spontaneously and repeatedly flush, along with all of the water turning on at full force from every faucet, including the bathtub. Each one of them had come running out of the bathroom, shaking and scared.

I told them I would take care of it. I stepped into the center of the bathroom, quietly standing there for a couple of minutes. My friends gathered outside the door, filling up the hallway and spilling into the kitchen to watch.

I looked around at the quiet bathroom, and in a loud, clear voice, I said, "I DON'T KNOW WHAT YOU WANT, BUT STOP SCARING MY FRIENDS! YOU NEED TO LEAVE THIS HOUSE, NOW!"

The words were barely out of my mouth when the fury was unleashed! Simultaneously, the toilet flushed; every faucet turned on full force, including the tub; and the valance and curtain on the window and the shower curtain came crashing to the floor—as though someone had grabbed them and ripped them down with force!

Everyone was still screaming as they grabbed their coats off my bed. I ran into the living room, profusely apologizing, trying to explain that there was definitely something wrong with the house, quietly adding that we would be moving shortly. I don't think any of them heard me, because there was practically a stampede out the front door.

I closed the door knowing that I couldn't wait for the owner to return from his trip. We would be out of this house as soon as humanly possible, no matter what. I lived in terror every day; my mother had been a nervous wreck since the police incident; and the last straw was them terrorizing my friends. We started looking for a new place the next day, and were moving ten days later.

The owner never asked me why we were moving, but he agreed to come over on the day of the move to collect the keys. The movers were loading the last pieces on the truck when he showed up. I told him to come into the house, but he refused. Instead he stood nervously in the driveway, sweating profusely. I walked up to him, standing uncomfortably close, asking him, "Who died in the back bedroom of that house?"

He stepped back, refusing to look at me, nervously saying, "I don't know what you're talking about."

I stepped forward and grabbed his lapel, pulling him close so he couldn't avoid looking in my eyes. "Stop lying, and tell me who died in that back room!"

Now he just looked scared. Sputtering and trying to pull out of my grasp, he twisted around, but I wouldn't let go. He stopped moving around when he realized that he wasn't going anywhere until he told me. He took a deep breath as he tried to look away, and as his shoulders slumped forward, he finally gave in, emotionless. "My aunts took every penny they had and built this house. Both of them died in it, in that back room."

Now it all made sense, but I wanted to know who they were and why they were still so attached to this house. "What did they do that they built that huge kitchen?" I let go of his lapel.

All of his fear faded as he finally let go of the lies connected to the house. "They were vaudeville dancers, and after that they did USO shows for the troops until they got sick. They entertained half of Hollywood, and as many of the armed forces as they could, in that house. It was their dream house."

I was so angry that he didn't tell me when we moved in. I looked at him and said, "Just so you know, they will keep terrorizing every person you rent their house to, until you rent it to people like them. They almost killed me!

So don't even think of renting it to anyone, unless it is a pair of sisters who are dancers, because they won't let anyone else live in their house in peace."

As I handed him the keys, I was grateful to find out the source of my four months of terror in this house, and to finally understand that the reason we had been chased out was because the vaudeville-dancing sisters had never really left.

Over the years I have driven by the house on Fountain a thousand times. I found out that the house had been sold to two sisters who were dancers on television.

The Chase

It was a rare comfort I felt that night in January 1978, as an unacknowledged fear softly lapped at the undercurrent of our lives in Los Angeles. Everyone was scared, with fear underlining the smiles. The city had been taken hostage by the unspeakable terror of an ongoing serial murder case. There didn't seem to be an end to the murders, and I understood why Angelenos were afraid; they had a reason to be. I knew that firsthand, because I had been working on these Hillside Strangler murders with the Los Angeles Police Department.

An impromptu evening at my friend Lisa's was exactly what I needed to try and take my mind off of the murders. It was a night filled with great barbecue, one of her exotic salads, a few nice friends, and lots of laughter. The night air was crisp, dark, and clear as the six of us stood outside counting stars, falling short of naming anything past the Big Dipper. We told corny jokes, drank lots of soft drinks, and gave in to the temptations of our abundantly filled plates. Music and laughter softly filled the air in her Los Feliz neighborhood as the hours slipped away, seemingly without a care, clinging to the safety of our friendships. I was grateful to be surrounded by people I trusted and loved. They provided a touchstone for me, a sense of safety and warmth.

We all laughed a lot that night—probably harder, longer, and louder than any of our silly jokes warranted, if only to mask the terror we carried inside. A tingling feeling crept up my neck as I fleetingly thought about the last few weeks of working with the police. I kept trying to shake the brutal images from my mind.

This was the most relaxed I had felt in weeks, and I didn't want to think about the murdered girls. I consciously pushed it to the back of my mind, making myself laugh out loud as I recalled some of the funny moments from this magical evening. I looked forward to going to sleep that night, my head filled with nothing but lovely memories.

The Hillside Strangler murders were happening all around us, within a mile from where we had innocently stood picking stars out of the carefree night sky. Women were being mutilated, murdered, and dumped by roadsides and on people's front lawns to be found. It was a terrifying thought that another serial killer was loose in Los Angeles. There had been others in Southern California over the years, but these murders were different.

The Hillside Strangler, as this murderer was dubbed, had tortured, raped, and murdered more than the nine dead women found. His reign of terror took strong, emancipated women and made them feel vulnerable for the first time in years. Their hard-earned freedom to go out for an evening in the city had been swept away with the final breath of the first victim.

Stories filled the daily headlines as fear-filled conversations were overheard everywhere. No one seemed to have the slightest idea about who was committing these heinous crimes, and unspoken questions hung like dew in the morning air: Where would he strike next? Was there a pattern aside from the killer's personal imprint on every lifeless body found? The police, along with everyone else in Los Angeles, were desperate for answers.

All of the victims had been young women with varying lifestyles, and the media's thinly veiled justification of the murders due to the victims' lifestyles certainly wasn't enough to pacify the women in Los Angeles. The savagery of the slayings was repeated endlessly, screaming out from every headline of every newspaper and vividly recounted on every newscast. We were continually assaulted by the gruesome details of the torture, and reminded of how seamlessly the killer moved from one victim to the next with complete anonymity.

Men felt completely helpless, as the killer had no face. He was a phantom, and men were left naked to defend the women they loved from this monster. It was a terrible time, as no one was safe in the City of Angels.

Always known as residents of one of the friendliest cities in the world, the people of Los Angeles stopped extending themselves. Even to each other. Markets, department stores, even gas stations, always crowded during the day, became wastelands the minute the sun went down. People simply stopped talking to each other. They stopped making eye contact, or even looking at each other, and it was the first time I had ever witnessed fear overtake an entire city.

This was a very painful case for me to work on. I had been contacted to work on the case by a liaison for the police department, and because the police were not used to consulting a psychic for anything, they didn't like this situation one bit. They made no attempt to hide their frustration at not having solved these murders already, or their utter lack of respect for my work and having to work with a psychic at all. Their attitude didn't stop me, because my intentions were very clear and had nothing to do with the police. For me it was about the girls, their families, and the city I grew up in. I wanted to help the girls who had been murdered to be able to rest. I wanted to help their families find as much peace as possible; and, if they would allow me to, I wanted to help the police get this monster off the street.

Much to my surprise, when I started to describe the Hillside Strangler, I saw that it was actually two men, not one. I described them and told the police that they were related, and that I saw them in a dark-colored van. I provided the police with several hours of taped details about the two men, telling them everything I saw. I described the area they lived in, the type of work they did, and two surprising details that had never been released to anyone in the media. The detectives were freaked out that I knew they thought the Hillside Strangler might be a cop, possibly one of their own. I assured them that neither one of these monsters were police officers, but the part that completely stunned them happened as I described in great detail the very specific injuries and wounds that had been found on the girls' bodies. Those even unnerved me.

As I left the party in Los Feliz, climbing into my car to head home, I was surprised to see that it was almost three in the morning. The night had flown by, and though I had stayed much later than usual, it was definitely worth it. I couldn't imagine anything marring the peace I felt in my heart. Not only was I wrong, but it almost cost me my life.

The streets were quiet as I slipped my car onto the freeway. It was really weird when I realized that I had the freeway all to myself. I had never seen it this empty, and after passing one other car going in the opposite direction, there wasn't another soul in sight. I picked up speed in a hurry to get home, thankful that I lived in Studio City and had a relatively short drive on the freeway to get there.

The night was so still. I turned the radio on for company, but just as quickly snapped it off. Suddenly I had that tingling on my neck again, and the creepiest feeling that I was being watched. My rational mind kicked in, and I thought how crazy that thought was. I was alone on the freeway. Who in the world could be watching me, and how? I tried to shake it off, but the feeling persisted.

I checked my rearview mirror, but the road was empty, not a headlight in sight. I glanced around the car, but no one was there. My heart beat faster as I leaned forward to look in my side-view mirror, catching a glimpse of something in the lane right next to me, hiding in my blind spot! It was a van, and they were keeping pace with me! I thought my heart was going to leap out of my chest.

I took a deep breath to calm myself down, rationalizing that they must have been there since I got on the freeway, and because I was tired, I simply hadn't noticed them. But where did they come from? I thought that I would just slow down and let them pass me, and that would be the end of this.

I took my foot off the accelerator, expecting them to whiz past me, but that is not what happened. They slowed down, dropping back to stay in my blind spot. I kept the slower speed as I leaned forward to get a better look at them in my side-view mirror. Looking closely at the van, I tried to talk myself out of what my heart already knew was true. It was the dark-colored van I had repeatedly described to the police over the last few weeks, and the driver and his passenger were the two men I had described as the Hillside Stranglers. They were the only people on the freeway with me, and had clearly been watching me and following me! Now I was completely terrified!

I continued staring at the face of the man in the passenger seat, jerking back into my seat as he looked directly at me in my side-view mirror. My heart was racing as I began crying out loud, pleading with God to help me. "Please, God, it isn't supposed to end this way. PLEASE, PLEASE, God, show me the way!"

Though my heart was still racing, I gripped the steering wheel as I loped along the freeway; now I was just trying to clear my mind. I had to come up with a plan to get myself out of this horrible situation, but I knew I wouldn't survive this unless I calmed the hysteria in my mind.

I quickly recalled all the safety lessons I had learned from the police over the years. I had learned how to defend myself if I was out alone at night, and how to keep myself out of harm's way, along with many other valuable tips. But a situation like this, where I was being chased on the freeway by two deranged, sadistic serial killers, had certainly never been addressed. There was no rule book or safety advice for this scenario. I was completely on my own.

Suddenly it was crystal clear, and I knew what I had to do. I vividly remembered advice I had heard long ago about what to do if someone was following you. Though my situation was a whole lot worse than that, at least it was a starting point. As I crept along the freeway, I realized we were still alone and there were no other cars. I had been driving in the middle lane and wasn't even close to an off-ramp, but I had to try and get away from them, and I only had one chance to do it.

I had to plan this out as precisely as I could under the circumstances. There were a thousand things running through my mind, but I only needed two elements for this to work. The first was that I had to do something completely unexpected, and the second and most critical point was that I had to make sure there was someplace that I could run in to for safety, a place that was very well lit, with people in it. The problem was that it was after three in the morning, and the city was pretty well closed up. I had to drive until I could figure out a place, close to one of the upcoming off-ramps, that had a parking lot at its front door. If I could solve that puzzle, then I could jump out and run inside. Now the trick was to keep an eye on the van while I figured out what business would be open at that hour.

I ran through the exits coming up in my head, racing through the places near each off-ramp. There was only one that I thought of that had everything I needed to save my life: the Vineland Avenue exit, and there was a convenience store two blocks away. I hoped that if I suddenly cut over and sped off the freeway that it might catch them off-guard. Since I thought their van was slower and more cumbersome than my car, I could outrun them. I figured if it worked, maybe I could lose them, and they would lose their opportunity to kill me.

The Vineland Avenue off-ramp was coming up fast. I didn't do anything until the last minute, when I gunned the engine, cut over two lanes, and flew down the off-ramp. I saw the red light at the bottom of the ramp, but I hoped for the first time in my life that a police car would be sitting on the street as I blew through the red light.

Just as I turned onto Vineland, I glimpsed the van's headlights in my rearview mirror: they had followed me off the freeway and were picking up speed. I was a block and a half away from the convenience store. All I had to do was go for it, turn the corner, and jump out of the car! Breathing heavily, I pushed as hard as I could to get there. Flying around the corner, I pulled up to the front door. I couldn't believe my eyes: the lot was empty and the store was closed!

I threw the car in gear, screeching out of the driveway, catching a glimpse of the van just as they turned the corner. They were fifty yards behind me as I sped down Ventura Boulevard without the slightest idea of where to run next, but I knew I'd better come up with something quick.

I was within blocks of my home, but my mother was living with me, so I had to keep them as far away from my house as possible. I was so panicked I could barely think. I looked in the rearview mirror to see they were still there.

I lived in a part of Studio City that had homes built on large lots; the area had originally been zoned for horse properties. They were lovely, quiet homes, but the street that I lived on had only one way in; it was a dead end. There was no way out.

I turned onto Colfax Avenue, making another quick right and speeding up to turn at the second street in. It was the only street that I could think of that was pitch-black at night, because it didn't have any streetlights. I drove a few houses in, killing my headlights as I pulled into the driveway of someone's house. I pulled as far back in the driveway as I could go, and as close to the house as I could get. I turned off my engine and hunkered down in my seat, twisting around to peek out to the end of the driveway.

My heart was pounding, and I was breathing so hard that I thought I was going to faint from hyperventilating. I was terrified, and they had been so persistent that, at this point, all I could do was hope that my breath wasn't fogging up the windows in case they had figured out where I was. I quietly started to pray under my breath, pleading once again with God.

I was frozen in place, peeking between the seats, when suddenly I saw headlights flooding the street. I held my breath as I watched the van slowly pull across the end of the driveway, with a handheld flashlight directed at the back of my car. They didn't move for what seemed like an eternity, moving the flashlight back and forth from the window of the van toward my car, but finally they crept past the driveway heading toward the dead end. I knew they would have to turn around to get out, and when they did, they slipped across the foot of the driveway, sitting there one more time, shining the flashlight in my direction, taking one last look before they left.

Though I was only a few blocks from home, I couldn't move. I was too terrified to take the chance that they might still be out there, waiting. I didn't move, staying curled up, peeking out between my seats, at the pitch-black street for at least thirty minutes after they were finally gone. I wanted to believe that they were far away before I felt safe enough to go home.

It was almost daylight when I walked in my front door. I poured myself a cup of coffee and was sitting at the dining room table when my mother took the seat across from me. I got up, walked around the table, and without a word I burst into tears as I put my arms around her and wouldn't let go. Though my mother knew that something terrible had happened to me that night, I could never bring myself to tell her; she didn't need to carry the burden of that knowledge.

The experience of that evening taught me invaluable lessons, and changed my life and my work in many ways. It took me a long time to get over the terror of seeing who I had described as the faces of the killers suddenly come to life, only to realize they were hunting me. Though it took time, I needed to understand the energy that had been operating that night, that made our paths cross. I realized that because I had openly and willingly worked on the Hillside Strangler murders, I had opened the door for that energy to enter my life. I realized that I had done absolutely nothing to spiritually protect myself from their destructive, violent energy.

Learning how to protect myself spiritually was a learned process, and it didn't happen overnight. When I first started giving readings professionally, I didn't understand nor was I fully aware of how another person's energy or issues could impact my life. I was open to everything, and without knowing that I needed to find what worked to keep me spiritually safe, I was highly vulnerable to the negative people and energies in my clients' lives.

Sometimes after finishing a reading, and without even realizing how it happened, I would have a health problem develop that I knew did not belong to me. After several doctors' visits to resolve whatever the issue was, I began to understand that I was vulnerable to absorbing the health issues of my clients and their loved ones, and I made a conscious effort to learn and utilize different practices for protection.

I have found that each person, whether they are involved in spiritual work or not, has their own way of protecting themselves from negative energies brought into their lives, or the lives of those around them. There isn't "one size fits all" when it comes to protecting yourself—and whether it is prayer, meditation, an amulet, or a variety of different practices, you have to find what feels right for you and your life, and that is what works.

Because of my close encounter with the Hillside Stranglers, I learned to spiritually protect my energy and myself, always. From this experience I have also become more careful about the murder cases I agree to work on, more sensitive to the residual darkness, and acutely aware of the negative baggage they may leave behind.

I am forever grateful that God heard my pleas for help that night, allowing me the opportunity to know what true evil looks like and to learn the value of protecting myself and others.

Conclusion

As I began to write the stories for *My Life Across the Table*, I didn't realize how deeply personal it would become to revisit the people, places, lessons, and emotions that I have shared over the years.

Every one of the readings and experiences I have shared with you profoundly inspired me, touched me, and changed my life in ways I could never have known.

Though I have changed all of my clients' names to protect their privacy, every one of the people, experiences, and stories in this book are true and hold a permanent place in my heart.

I hope you enjoy the stories I have chosen to share, and that in some small way they can convey the impact and importance of the work on a psychic's life.

I live in gratitude every day for having been entrusted and blessed with an extraordinary gift and living this amazing life.

I hope you enjoyed *My Life Across the Table*, and I hope you will take a moment to visit my website at www.KarenPage.com. Please sign my guestbook and let me know you came by.

Acknowledgments

There are so many people I am grateful to have in my life, for a million different reasons, and most certainly without them *My Life Across the Table* would never have happened.

This is but a small portion of the people who have nurtured my soul throughout the years. I am grateful for their profound kindness, their amazing minds, their never-ending talents, and their boundless love, friendship, and support.

I can't imagine a day of my life without you, so if ever for a moment you wonder ... I thank you from my heart.

My wonderful friend, the amazing playwright Yussef El Guindi, for the ongoing encouragement to write, which has nourished my soul for the last twenty-five years. Thank you from my heart.

My incredibly talented friend Mark Rivett, an amazing composer and producer, for his warmth, patience, laughter, lunch, and support in recording *My Life Across the Table*. Thank you from my heart.

My dearest friend, Warren Weideman, for your never-ending kindness, love, pies, incredibly hard work, creativity, and sheer genius, and for really "getting me" from the moment we met. Thank you from my heart.

My wonderful friend Peter Giagni, for your friendship, perseverance, hard work, and your most beautiful heart. Thank you from my heart.

My wonderful and loving friend Chris Chekel, for your beautiful friendship, your enormous heart, and your amazing mind, and most of all for your deeply appreciated kindness. Thank you from my heart.

My wonderful and loving Mark Shamash, for your endless creativity, your beautiful and loving heart, your never-ending kindness, your brilliant mind, the most interesting conversations, my beautiful photograph…and above it all, just for being you. Thank you from my heart.

My beautiful friend Tracy Balsz, for your generous nature, your deeply appreciated hard work, your loving support and creativity, and the warmth of your beautiful spirit. Thank you from my heart.

My beautiful friend Marci Merliss-Holliday, for your enormous heart, your endless kindness, and twenty-five years of laughter and support. Thank you from my heart.

My creative pixie Linda Faun Sherman, for your joyful soul, your loving heart, and the true gift of friendship and sisterhood. Thank you from my heart.

I would also like to thank the tens of thousands of people who have been **Across the Table** from me. Thank you from my heart.

To Write to the Author

If you wish to contact the author or would like more information about this book, please write to the author in care of Llewellyn Worldwide Ltd. and we will forward your request. Both the author and publisher appreciate hearing from you and learning of your enjoyment of this book and how it has helped you. Llewellyn Worldwide Ltd. cannot guarantee that every letter written to the author can be answered, but all will be forwarded. Please write to:

Karen Page
℅ Llewellyn Worldwide
2143 Wooddale Drive
Woodbury, MN 55125-2989

Please enclose a self-addressed stamped envelope for reply, or $1.00 to cover costs. If outside the USA, enclose an international postal reply coupon.